Paul Elmer More

The Great Refusal

Being letters of a dreamer in Gotham

Paul Elmer More

The Great Refusal
Being letters of a dreamer in Gotham

ISBN/EAN: 9783337015718

Printed in Europe, USA, Canada, Australia, Japan

Cover: Foto ©ninafisch / pixelio.de

More available books at **www.hansebooks.com**

THE GREAT REFUSAL

BEING

LETTERS OF A DREAMER
IN GOTHAM

EDITED BY

PAUL ELMER MORE

" Amanti verbum non mundum "

BOSTON AND NEW YORK
HOUGHTON, MIFFLIN AND COMPANY
The Riverside Press, Cambridge
1894

The Riverside Press, Cambridge, Mass., U. S. A.
Electrotyped and Printed by H. O. Houghton & Co.

INTRODUCTION

ALL that is necessary for the understanding of these letters can be told in a few words. Their author was born and educated in New York. After receiving the baccalaureate degree at Columbia College, he studied in the graduate classes for two years, and then went abroad. He traveled through the various countries of Europe, passing a winter in Greece, and proceeded thence to India and the far East, where he remained a number of months. He would have been content, on returning home, to give himself up to a life of leisure and quiet study, as the means of his family permitted; but the American instincts of his father and relatives in general regarded such unproductive idleness as degrading. In accordance with their wishes, he overcame his reluctance, and accepted a position as teacher in the —— school, this being the only active life he deemed himself suited to enter upon. Here he fulfilled the duties of instructor in Latin for one year, but I am told the result was deplorable. The nervous strain was too great for his sensitive nature, and by spring-time his health was so materially affected that he was permitted to retire from active life and bury himself in his study. He never, after that, left his home on Staten Island, except to visit in the city. And his learning, which even at this age must have been prodigious, was wasted in the vapors of mysticism.

It was in the early spring of his year of misfortune, and under circumstances described in one of these letters, that he met the woman whom he chose to call Lady Esther. Her influence over him can be gathered from the following pages.

I myself saw him twice at her house. His appearance was noticeable enough. On the street, perhaps, one would have passed him by without a second look, but in the parlor his attitude and the expression of his countenance marked him at once as a man apart. He was rather tall, and of a slender figure, quick but not ungraceful in movement. His head was large and high ; but what impressed one most was the peculiar lack of harmony between the lower and upper parts of his face. His mouth and chin were soft, almost voluptuous, the curve of the lips wavering between melancholy and sarcasm. The eyes, on the other hand, were cold, abstracted, and repellent. They were the eyes of a dreamer, but of an egotist as well. I remember one occasion when the sympathetic expression of the mouth and the distant, abstracted look of the eyes made a contrast that had about it something almost preternatural.

Again, a third time, not long before his death, I met him in his own home under circumstances peculiarly trying. It was shortly after the last letter in this collection was written, and when he had completely withdrawn himself from the world in order to follow out certain oriental notions concerning the spiritual life. I was the bearer of a message of the utmost delicacy. He received me cordially, with the precise and impressive manner habitual to men who pass their time among books, and I think divined at once the reason of my visit. For the sake of privacy, perhaps, he led me into his library, a large rectangular room on the second floor, from whose windows I could see the sparkling water of the bay, and afar off the smoke of the great city. I observed here, for the first time in my life, the subduing, almost melancholy, effect of the view of many vessels passing silently before our gaze. The room itself was plainly furnished, with bookshelves built against the walls and reaching almost to the ceiling. Several large photographs from the Buddhist monasteries, and a watercolor representing our friend, were the only pictures; indeed, his books left little space for ornaments. Only one object struck me as at all bizarre: on the mantel was a carefully mounted death's-head, with a short inscription in crimson paint across the forehead. The characters were Sanscrit, as I suspected.

Our conversation soon turned to oriental subjects suggested by the Buddhist scenes on the wall, and from them I took occasion to refer to the portrait, remarking the excellence of the likeness. He assured me it was done from a small photograph by an artist who had never seen the original, but who was guided by his directions. He spoke of her quite freely, of her astonishing beauty, and of the influence she had formerly exercised on his character. I was encouraged by his frankness to express my surprise that he should find it necessary, in pursuance of his conception of the higher life, to abandon this influence which even yet awakened in him such noble reflections. He replied at some length, as if anxious to render my task easy.

"There is a state in our progress," he said, " when nothing is more efficacious in arousing our purest sentiments and leading us upward, than the contemplation of beauty. This seems to us then the divine light sent into the world to guide our steps in slippery places. The man who follows it is a Platonist. You have read the ' Phædrus ' and the ' Symposium,' and I need say no more. But as time goes on, we are dismayed to find our advance checked at a certain point beyond which this guide cannot take us. Then our perception is deepened. The material world is seen in its naked reality. Two paths are open to us. Either with the followers of the Vedanta we look upon

matter as pure illusion, arising out of ignorance
and ready to vanish away as soon as comprehended: or else, with the school of the Sankhya,
we deem it eternal and self-existent; but still
look upon the union of the spirit with it as the
result of illusion and ignorance, which being removed, the spirit escapes from its fetters, and
Nature, as a dancing girl who has once been seen,
retires modestly from view. Pardon my reference to unfamiliar philosophies, but I do not
know how better to express that stage of our
spiritual progress when the material world becomes in every aspect a hindrance to us. Which-
ever way our reason leads us — and the two
systems are morally one — beauty to the enlightened mind becomes above all things the most
dangerous illusion. Were it not for the beautiful forms of Nature displayed before the soul,
we should not cling to our present impure state,
nor refuse to accept in its fullness the divine
light already perceived by the intellect."

"But," I objected, "is there nothing besides
this? Can you not conceive of moral excellence
in another which might still make love a celestial
guide in this higher life, without appealing to
mere physical beauty?"

"You miss my meaning. There is no moral
excellence, as you understand it. Such qualities
of the heart are still connected with manners
and physical agents. The true aim of the phi-

losopher is not morality, in this sense, but isolation and inattachment, if I may use the word.
Though I grant you in the first stages of our
growth moral excellences are a help to the spirit,
and love may be the greatest promoter of these;
yet, later on, love itself becomes a drag on our
progress. From the individual we extend this
love to our neighbors, from them to the world at
large in ever widening circles. This is Christian
charity, the highest law for him who may be called
the secular man. But beyond this there is a state,
plainly propounded even in Christian works such
as the 'Imitation,' in which we strive to loose
ourselves from all attachment whatsoever. When
this is accomplished, the soul is made fit for
readmission into God. From the realm of law
to the realm of spirit is a painful but necessary step. To one not well prepared, it may
even be a most dangerous step, utterly overturn-
ing the basis of his character, and perhaps leading him into a life not of non-morality but of
gross immorality. Herein, I think, lies the explanation of the scandals that so often creep into
mystical sects. But to him who is prepared, love,
just in so far as it is attached to what is fair,
becomes a more serious obstacle. We must
renounce.   But do not suppose it has cost me
nothing to refuse " —

"Why," I cried out, "this is no less than *il
gran rifiuto*, the great refusal!"

"And you might add," he continued, smiling,

"that he who makes it is fit neither for heaven
nor for hell, as the poet declares. Yet have you
not read the legend of the fanatic who ran
through the streets of Byzantium with a torch in
one hand and a vessel of water in the other, crying aloud that with this torch he would set fire to
heaven, and with this water he would quench
hell, that henceforth men might worship God
alone? As for me, what matters it? —

'Nam mihi parta quies, omnisque in limine portus;
Funere felici spolior.'"

"That is well," I said, and looking upon him
I seemed to see, even then, the mark of death
on his brow; "that is well; but think of the
woman. It may be"—

He interrupted me, divining what I was about to
say. "Perhaps it was just because I began to see
what you would suggest, that I acted so suddenly
and decisively. Perhaps it was better so.—
And after all, Mr. More," he continued with the
evident intention of turning aside a conversation
that had grown painful to us both, "what does
it signify? The motto on yonder death's-head
might warn us that we are wasting words, you
and I. You do not know Sanscrit, I presume;
but if you did you would read there the profoundest
maxim in the world, the mystic symbol, *that art
thou.* The words have a wide application and
may inculcate the purest spirituality or the
basest materialism; but always they must stand
as a reproof for idle regrets."

It had grown late. I had said what I could, very little perhaps, but words seemed quite ineffectual; and rose to leave. At his urgent request, however, I remained to take tea with him, which he had served in the same room. His conversation interested me extremely, having that peculiar flavor which results from long seclusion and profound introspection. Yet the final impression on me was something akin to sadness, and it was a relief when I left him and passed out into the clear atmosphere of a winter night.

I never saw him again, and only learned of his death some months afterwards when these letters were put into my hands to edit. The task was not ungrateful to me, for with all their mystical impracticability they may yet withdraw some of us for an hour at least from our sordid workaday life; and it may not be unprofitable to learn that such a character has been amongst us and dreamed his dreams amid the turmoil of the great city. The letters are all to one person, the lady who was our friend, and were written generally from his home after returning from her house in the evening. I think any one will understand the delicate feeling which has led her to give them to the world. My work as editor has been simply to select. Very little had to be omitted in order to carry out the one injunction laid upon me, that all names and recognizable allusions should be suppressed. P. E. M.

CAMBRIDGE, November 16, 1893.

THE GREAT REFUSAL

BEING

LETTERS OF A DREAMER IN GOTHAM

I.

A SONNET to Mistress Esther ———, on her com-
plaining of growing indifference to the world and
lack of enthusiasm ; wherein her Spirit is likened
unto a Planet giving light to others, while unto
itself seeming quite dark ; for such is the disposition of the wandering stars, and such comparison her name Esther suggests : and admonition
is added that she do not regret the new tranquil-
lity of her life, whose action is best likened unto
the serene motion of that same Planet.   Composed by me the seventeenth day of July, 1890,
and transmitted to the fair Subject on the day
following, to whom also greeting.

Fear not, sweet Lady, for thy heart's repose !
   I, looking on thy spirit from afar,
   Behold it as these eyes discern a star,
   Whose radiant glory to all others flows,
Though to itself quite dark ; which neither knows
   The motion of a path no tumults jar,
   Nor in what hands the reins ethereal are
   That guide it in the orbit where it goes.

So be the wonder of thy life to hold
  Serenely as a planet its fair way
Of cloudless light, by heavenly laws controlled :
Such bonds unfelt thy track harmonious sway
  Where purer orbs their web of peace unfold
  To clothe our spirit-night in sweet array.

II.

On returning home last evening I found the air cooled by a local shower from the clouds which, you remember, alarmed us while on the bay. Trees and shrubs were still dripping, and the dust had disappeared. If you had been on Staten Island lately and seen its parched condition, you would understand how this little madrigal came into my head. As for its interpretation, let the wise friend who is with you expound that together with any other conundrums the day may have suggested. It is tragical, comical, or melodramatic, as you choose.

  Dripping from leaf to leaf
  The raindrops bring relief
And cool from cloudy cisterns whence they ooze.
  Oh that celestial dews,
  Dropping within my breast,
  After the burning passion might infuse
  Freshness like this, and rest !

III.

. . . But I take this occasion to send an apology for that taciturn behavior last night which brought down on me your heavy rebuke. It seemed to me that in the din of so much chatter my silence would not be observed : and then too from my drowsy corner among your luxurious cushions, I looked out over the trees into the sky ; and the sight of the planet Jupiter, sailing like a silver shallop over the undulating treetops, acted upon me as a spell. He had just crossed the meridian when I bade you good-night.

> Chide not, sweet Lady, if at times
>   Silent I sit in pensive mood ;
>   It may be then my heart would brood
> Praise unto thee in ordered rhymes.
>
> It may be, while I sat absorbed
>   In quietude thou deem'dst a slight,
>   It was the solemn hush of night
> Lulling the wide sky many-orbed.
>
> And while I watched that planet roll,
>   Dreaming, thou saidst, of things afar,
>   Thy Spirit wandered like that star
> Across the vistas of my soul.

IV.

The humblest of my Lady's servants will be delighted to attend her Tuesday evening. As to our discussion about the fair Venus of Milo, from which side one gets the better view of her, — well, he has elaborated a strong argument on that head from the position of the statue in reference to the light, and from other recondite considerations which may astound a certain obstinate critic.

Friday night, being exceedingly disconsolate because of his great disappointment, he attempted to solace himself, as is his wont, with one of the Muses, who never, never is *not-at-home.* She poured many kind words into his ear ; and he would gladly repeat them if considerations of prudence did not admonish silence. However, the inclosed fragment may do no harm. The lady to whom the verses are addressed may be amazed at their utter lack of veracity, but let her consider that the muse has methods of her own, not to be judged by the impertinent canons of reality. Moreover, the muse dwells in a small and dark chamber (whether it be the heart or the brain is not certainly determined), and can express herself only on what is reported to her from the outer world. Now at times certain desires are so domineering that the poor muse is utterly at loss to distinguish between the real

action and the desire of action, for the continual
and deafening hubbub which this desire raises in
her ladyship's narrow cell.   Therefore it may be
the chivalrous knight in question did not act in so
romantic a manner as the muse relates in these
verses.   But who shall say what desire of desires
stirred his breast when the goddess of his vows appeared before him in the flesh,

"Virginis os habitumque gerens,"

perfect and without mutilation, fairer perhaps
than her marble image — who shall say ?

Hear, at least, what the muse hath to speak.

> To heal the feud between us
> My Lady posed for Venus,
> From whether side to shew
> One had the better view.
> And I, ah well, I humbly bent the knee
> And kissed her marble hand,
> Bewildered quite to see
> The goddess all complete before me stand,
> The fair Parisian Venus
> Who wrought the feud between us.

V.

Has it ever happened to you carelessly to enter
a room where you were met at the threshold by
some strange feeling of unreality and mysticism,
as if an unseen presence were abiding within?

Perhaps it was the uncertain light which impressed you so, or a familiar odor, or some trivial object which met your eye and brought to your mind confused reminiscences. If so, you will appreciate what happened to me yesterday; and the little madrigal inclosed herewith may give you the pleasure of one of those rare moments when the past and present seem mingled together in a delightful dream. — I chanced to enter a parlor when the level rays of the sun, floating in through the heavy lace curtains, flooded the room with indescribable sweetness. The carpet was one of those dull blue velvets worked with curious Persian designs which always appear to mean more than the eye can detect. The tremulous light falling on these emblems gave them just that uncertainty of outline needed to transform them into the figures of a dream. At the window, to catch the last glow of the day, was a chair, and on it an open book, face down, — a copy of Propertius, as I found. Evidently the reader whom I awaited had just fled. On the floor were scattered a few wilted day-lilies. They are a fragile flower, with their delicate purple corolla like a painted vase, and the long, protruding stamens, which in these specimens were drooping over the pale lips of the chalice. Altogether, you will see that not without reason I started at the threshold, as if about to enter a place of faerie. And when I sat

down in the vacant chair and looked at the open
page of the volume, my dream was not dispelled
by the words that first caught my eye : —

"Multi longinquo periere in amore libenter."

Absit omen! I whispered, and closed the book.
You are fond of Propertius, are you not?

> The tremulous sunlight lay
> Dreamily on the floor,
> Weaving the colors of the dying day
> The Persian emblems o'er;
> While odors, as of one just gone away,
> Hovered about the door.
> And on the carpet scattered,
> The purple petals lay
> Of lilies-of-a-day,
> As if in all that house to none it mattered
> That these were cast away.
> Over their purple lips
> The stamens lolled for breath,
> As from the pallid mouth of one who sips
> The languid draught of death.
> And there I dreamed my dream
> Of love and lilies, while the last pale beam
> With kisses cherished, ere it crept away,
> These flowers of but a day.

VI.

You have asked me several times how I came
to seek out your acquaintance, and I am tempted

at last to tell you. Will you be surprised to hear that the beauty and grace of your brother first attracted me, and that, too, in the school-room? I cannot express to you how much his face meant to me through those dreary months of teaching. One fair object can redeem a whole landscape, and one sentiment of delight can make a barren year endurable. If it had not been for him I should have suffered defeat long before the term ended. Naturally, when I heard of you, his sister, curiosity, if nothing else, led me to ask for your acquaintance. And must I add that this something else endured after curiosity was satisfied? Strangely enough, just before meeting you, I had seen a wonderfully radiant lady pass by the burial ground of Old Trinity, in whose enclosure I chanced then to be. Like one smitten by a vision of new beauty, I followed her only to lose her in the crowd of Broadway. It may be the trouble caused in my heart by that vision of the street acted on my dreamy enthusiasm for your brother and aroused me to action. At any rate, I sought you out and found, as deeper insight would have suggested, that you and the lady of my vision were one.

I send you a poem herewith, long and tedious perhaps, but which was inspired by one so close to you that you may claim it as your own — dullness and all.

THE PEDAGOGUE.

" In that same city of tremendous night."

I hear the sound of eager feet
Grow dimmer down the homeward street;
And boyish calls of merry tone
Come fainter now and leave me quite alone.

Awhile I tarry in the room,
Where silence falls with solemn gloom; —
And all that life, so linked with mine,
Is scattered here and there like drops of wine!

I wander down the empty form,
And pause beside his seat yet warm,
And stretch my hand as if to touch   .
The bended head of him I love so much.

But yesterday I stood above
And watched him, yearning in my love;
He saw, and faltered in the file,
And dropt his eyes, and answered smile with
      smile.

And once on leaving late he cried,
Now Bonus Nox! in boyish pride :
I caught him then and held him long,
And, holding, chided for the gender wrong.

O eyes undimmed by bookish dust!
O eyes unmarred by turbid lust!
That still behold me where I go
Amid the shadow-tides of ebb and flow.

For when the hours of school are o'er,
A sight or sound, unmarked before,
Can lure the spirit from its home
Far in the dusky shadow-world to roam.

Perchance to-day one sombre line,
Heard in a poem half malign,
Like a strange spell hath sent my soul
To find its far-off melancholy goal.

And there on either road among
The surging listless-footed throng,
He still is with me at my side,
And holds my hand, and looks up wonder-eyed.

And if at times I feel him shiver,
It is the chilling of this river
That past us rolls, whose every wave
Is but an errant soul in mantle grave.

For now our sloping steps descend
To that great Town where both ways end, —
The paths where homeward-journeying souls
Jostle the phantom-tide that with them rolls.

Here, too, the wayward spirits wander,
The seers of old, who dared to ponder,
Within the human hours of hope,
The darker truth beyond all mortal scope.

Wearily, back and forth they tread
This dusty highway of the dead,
Seeking among the languid shades
The alluring image that all search evades.

Others may find within the walls,
Far-off, where hope and anguish falls,
In dull forgetfulness a home ;
These for their knowledge must forever roam.

These in the hours of human hope,
Wandered into that City's scope,
And living drew its fateful breath ;
In vain they only crave its peace in death.

And one of these low in my ear
Whispers : What learning brings thee here ?
What knowledge that the God defends,
Brings thee to travel where all wisdom ends ?

Another plucks me by the sleeve :
O Brother ! if thy heart can grieve,
Go not this way ; behold it tends
Where all the yearning of the ages ends !

And one more surly mutters grim :
What hard ambition then leads him
With this sad caravan that wends
Where all desire and all ambition ends ?

Another grasping seeks to hold :
If grief and knowledge make thee bold,
Ah well! yet say what sorrow sends
This tender youth where all emotion ends ?

And all the while the way leads down
Unto that barricadoed town
Of death.   Behold the high-arched stone
Whose valves swing inward to receive alone !

I lean against the dusty gate,
And urge it open with my weight :
We enter and I whisper him,
Loose not thy tenure, for the light is dim.

And so we wander up the street;
And at the clamor of our feet
Strange echoes rise reluctantly,
And flit before us, where — we can not see.

Ah, who has entered by this gate
Is moved no more by love or hate :
Ah, who has visited this city
Feels in his heart no pulse of human pity.

Ah, who has trained the unused sight
To hunt blind shapes in this half-light,
Sees in the sky nor sun nor stars,
But spectres borne aloft in flaming cars.

And evermore he threads the world
A pilgrim with his mantle furled ;
And all he sees or hears but seems
The idle pageants of swift-passing dreams.

And if at intervals arise
Faint echoes of the old surprise
And passion, 't is a vagrant ghost
Haunting his ancient long-abandoned post.

For here within these city walls
No sound of laughter ever falls,
No tread of home-returning feet
Resounds along the melancholy street.

On either hand tall houses rise
With dead or heavy-slumbering eyes,
With dusty doors that never turn,
And smokeless chimneys where no fires may burn.

Within these walls no soul may be,
No soul of all humanity ;
And all these mansions ranging dumb
Stand always ready, yet no tenants come.

For when the spirit enters there,
Like smoke 't is scattered in the air:
Only their sighs that reach no ears,
Only the misty vapor of their tears,

Only the sobs of voiceless grief
Of this sad people past relief,
Remaining, cloud the air with pity,
Like fogs that overhang a human city.

And the dark sorrow of each heart
That with his life will not depart,
Here as a guilty thing abides,
And wanders wailing with the phantom-tides.

Dear boy, I whisper, close thy lips ;
For he who of this pestilence sips,
Sucks in his breast a weary weight
No laughter of the world will e'er elate.

Then he who walketh at my side
Looks up at me all wonder-eyed,
And questions, Of this desolate city
Where doth the Lord abide withouten pity ?

Ask not to see him, O my boy !
For in his eyes that know not joy,
And on his forehead, graven stern,
A judgment dwells thy heart must not discern.

But hist ! what murmur down the street
Of many lisping listless feet ?
It is the Lord of all our sighs ;
O boy, here in my mantle hide thine eyes.

I muffle in my scholar's gown
The frighted eyes, while drifting down
The highway comes the fluttering throng,
And midst them He to whom all tears belong.

We crouch within an empty door
Until the ghostly press is o'er ; —
Like shadows, when the wind is swift,
From swinging lanterns, down the street they
    drift.

I know whereto the current tends,
Within what walls their riot ends ;
And thither where the way is large
An evil fate impels me with my charge.

And lo, what ancient stones arise !
What latticed pinnacles pierce the skies !
The front like pointed lace is seen
With many a weird device by the dull sheen.

And round the eaves there frets and toils
The tortured race of gaunt gargoyles ;
Along the buttressed walls they slide
Wildly as only demon forms can glide.

We pause beneath the high-arched door
To view the patrons sculptured o'er;
And horror smites me lest he see
These wardens watching here eternally.

They are the dark things of the world,
Standing with mantle round them furled;
The woes, the sins, the nameless crime,
Standing like saints above these doors sublime.

Then in the sombre aisle aloof
We walk beneath the lofty roof,
Upon whose groinèd vaults the flare
Of the wan candles flickers cold and bare.

O boy, I whisper, close thine ears;
For he who of this worship hears,
Never within his soul may know
The love of God wherefrom all faiths do flow.

And He to whom all doubts belong,
Chants now before the silent throng
The word of words of blasphemy —
O love of truth, that ever such should be!

Out of an infinite curst desire,
As smoke arises out of fire,
A world of uncontrolled distress
Floats blindly through the deeps of nothingness.

He ends, and from their hollow throats
Rises the dull response, and floats
In dying cadences away;
While all that hushed assembly kneel to pray.

O boy, I whisper, if they kneel,
Bow not with them; for they appeal
Out of the depths of hellish woe
And dark remorse thy heart may never know.

Then He to whom all deaths belong,
Before the reverential throng
Lifts high the mystic sacrament,
While every head in silent awe is bent.

O boy, I whisper, close thine eyes,
For in his hands he doth comprise
The consummation of our shame,
The fearful sacrament no lips can name.

It is not to our bread allied,
'T is Jesus whom we crucified;
The very blood of God they sip,
And munch his very flesh with greedy lip.

For when the dead Christ entered hell,
They bound him in a fatal spell;
And we on earth in symbols make
The dread communion they in sooth partake.

And in the sorrow of his spirit
A strange existence they inherit ;
Yet when is all devoured his heart,
This phantom-world itself will melt apart.

Now wakes in slow solemnity
The hollow-toned antiphony
From nave and choir, and o'er their heads
Moanings and lamentable sobbing sheds.

And never in the light above,
And never in the world of love,
The soul that hears this lost complaint
Shall know the voice of human merriment.

And all the while in torment dumb,
Out of the black triforium,
Down on the awed assembly stared
A cloistered brood with eyes that burned and
    glared.

Out of the rayless gloom they leered,
With countenances scathed and bleared,
Feeding with scowls and mad sarcasms
The pain that writhed their lips in voiceless
    spasms.

O God ! that ever such should be,
Even in this haunt of misery !
And yet I know not which was worse,
The cringing homage or the scoffing nurse.

Woe's me! what fascination drew
Mine eyes to welter in that view ?
And the boy, noting then my dread,
Looked upward too and, seeing, fell as dead.

Down on the stones he fell outright,
His young heart silenced at the sight;
And at the rumor of such fall,
Unwonted here, a panic swept o'er all.

From either aisle and choir and nave,
Like waters rolling wave on wave,
They streamed in sudden flight away,
In terror heeding not where the boy lay.

Over his body low I bend,
And round him my long cloak extend,
And chafe his temples cold as death,
And vainly warm his nostrils with my breath.

And all the while with ceaseless surge
The hateful phantoms past us urge,
Heaving like billows on the floor,
And wildly tossing to the western door.

Yet saw I not the forms that beat
Tumultuously at our feet;
For the concussion of his fall
Had quenched the lights, and darkness shrouded
    all.

But oh, in agony I bowed
Over his face to stem the crowd !
And when at length the storm had flown,
Still o'er him bended, motionless as stone.

Darkness and silence reigned around,
A dreary darkness, vast, profound,
Save in the vaulted choir afar
One hanging censer burned, a crimson star ;

Save from the leaden-soldered crypt
Beneath the altar sadly slipt
A wavering sound, but half a sigh —
It was the weary Christ who would not die.

Still o'er the languid form I crouch,
But the dear eyes and lips avouch
No sign of life ; and the cold stones
Are sucking slow the warmth of flesh and bones.

And then my heart sinks utterly :
O Thou, I shriek, whoe'er thou be,
Where'er within this gloom thou lurk,
Shunning a mortal's eye for this thy work ;

Blind Power ! or shall I call thee worse ?
Haunting unseen this universe,
Give back this soul awhile to me,
Spare him awhile from thine eternity !

Then beaten from the stone-deaf walls
And vaulted roof the echo falls,
And as in mockery slowly trails
Down the long corridor in fitful wails.

And when at last this murmur stopt,
Thick silence as a curtain dropt;
And in the gloom where'er I turned,
Only that crimson censer dimly burned.

It seemed to me with gaze malign
Like as an evil eye to shine,
The only token of the Might
Haunting the wide intolerable night.

And from the leaden-soldered crypt
Beneath the altar sadly slipt
A wavering prayer, but half a sigh,
As if the weary Christ were fain to die.

And then a madness rent my heart
Out of this damnèd place to part,
To drag my charge, I knew not where,
Out of this limbo to the purer air.

Swift in my cloak I wrapt him round,
And bore him lightly from the ground,
And to my heart his cold heart pressed,
But felt no stirring in his silent breast.

Over my shoulders, limp and cold
Hung his fair head, and in my hold
He lay as one foredone by death,
Unwitting of my love, cold, without breath.

And so I sped across the floor;
But when I reached the western door,
Ah me! the valves were stoutly locked
With iron wards that every effort mocked.

Then in my frenzy groping there
I found a narrow winding stair,
As in the stone a snake were coiled:
Here, with my burden, upward slow I toiled.

And ever upward as I crept,
My sleeve along the rough wall swept
With a low melancholy sound,
That made the brooding stillness more profound.

And dropping down the dismal shaft
Upon us blew a noisome draft,
Whose heavy breath and clammy taint
Made the heart stagger in me, sick and faint.

Ah, sick and dizzy so I wend:
It seems the spiral ne'er will end!
And the sweet load, so light before,
Now weighs me down, and burdens more and
    more.

And, stumbling once, almost I fall,
And panting, lean against the wall;
And o'er my charge disconsolate bow,
Kissing his passive lips and marble brow :

Until the frenzy wakes once more,
And on I struggle as before ;
Until the bitter way is past,
And on the utmost tower I stand at last.

There might I rest, but from the city
The sodden air, surcharged with pity,
Hung round us in a sullen cloud,
Folding the tower within its vaporous shroud.

Sure it was poison to the breath,
And he, if ever won from death,
Where now his spirit toiled in fear,
Must breathe, I knew, a purer atmosphere.

Sheer from our very feet did rise
The slender spire into the skies ;
And through its latticed masonry
Upward the stairway wound laboriously.

And ever, as I climbed above,
Bearing my weary weight of love,
Steeper the steps and narrower grew,
Till, with my burden, scarce I clambered through.

And often as the spiral filed
Between the ribs of stone up-piled,
My heart grew faint to see the world
So far below us like a scroll unfurled.

And, gazing out into the night,
My vision blinded at the sight,
Where the thick air, surcharged with pity,
Rolled its voluminous smoke up from the city.

And once I staggered with his weight,
And almost fell precipitate,
Dizzy at heart; and crouching there
Rested a while in unforeseen despair.

O child, I murmured, in my arms
Sleep peacefully out of all harms!
And then with mingled fear and love
Kissing his eyes, I rose and toiled above.

And now I knew the atmosphere
Grew fresher as we mounted here:
And now I stood where the winds toss
Untinctured round the high-uplifted cross.

There, on the pinnacle, alone,
Beneath the very cope of stone,
Under the symbol of God's woe,
We pause, where the free winds of heaven blow.

O boy, I murmur, open fair
Thine eyes upon this sea of air ;
If it may be, unseal thy mouth
To drink new vigor after the long drouth.

Behold the pestilence of the city,
Its heavy breath surcharged with pity,
Spread as a cloud, beneath us churns ;
While all about the starry cosmos turns !

Ah me, the combat of the soul
Winning again its lost control !
Out of the regions vast of night
Once more in its old home usurping right !

The eyelids flutter wearily,
The pupils are distent to see,
And fitfully is drawn the breath,
While the soul wrestles with the tyrant Death.

'T is over, and I whisper soft :
O boy, for wonder look aloft ;
Surely we stand in the mid-sky
Whither each sun and planet turns its eye.

Out of the city's great despair
Rises this spire into the air ;
And wrought upon its summit, lo !
The eternal symbol of God's death and woe.

Behold, the ways of every star
Circle about this point afar;
And always, as they whirl through space,
Hither in awe and fear they turn their face.

Yonder like flaming fatui
They reel bewildered through the sky;
And sadly to each other call:
Turn faster, brother, lest we thither fall!

And we, O boy, we stand beneath
This fearful symbol of God's death;
And far below the city lies,
And over us the illimitable skies.

. . . .

Thus when the hours of school are o'er,
A sight or sound, unmarked before,
Can lure the spirit from its home
Far in the dusky shadow-world to roam.

And mid the surging ebb and flow
Of phantoms which no respite know,
He still is with me at my side,
And holds my hand, and looks up wonder-eyed.

And the strange visions of the night,
And broodings of our waking sight,
Greet us upon these ways that wend
Where all our thought and all our dreaming end.

VII.

. . . It is possible the following verses with their commentary may awaken in your mind the pleasant memory of a similar experience : for it is true, is it not, that all these moments of happier inspiration are wonderfully alike, linked together in such wise as to form a hidden life within our life ?   When we enter its secret precincts we know that we have been there before ; we breathe more lightly ; the vulgar every-day world is forgotten ; and we are prone to deem the communion of these sweeter moments, so blended together by memory, our only true existence after all.   " For life is but a dream whose shapes return."   Therefore, I say, these verses may awaken in you the recollection of some such vanished moment of inspiration.   Or, should I rather say that to me are granted intervals like these, while to thee, —

" Thou liest in Abraham's bosom all the year ;
    And worship'st at the Temple's inner shrine,
    God being with thee when we know it not " ?

Last Sunday night, if you recollect, the moon was full, and fairer even than usual.   I chanced to be out walking, and found myself in a road running east and west through the woods.   The moon, just then rising, hung wonderfully bright where the road, one might say, climbed from a long upward slope into the very heavens. The light, streaming in waves down this path between the trees, rolled past me like a great silvery river that flows silently among green hills. It was all very beautiful, you may fancy. At the time, however, it made little impression on me, as I was thinking of other things. But yesterday evening, after leaving your house, I walked down the avenue to my ferry. You know I was not in the cheerfulest of moods, and it seemed the sky sympathized with me more than certain human creatures had cared to do; for a thick mist covered the stars, and the moon barely gleaming therethrough looked pale and sad. But as I walked on dejectedly, suddenly the recollection of what I had observed Sunday flashed on my inner eye more vivid than at the actual occurrence. You will understand me when I say that for a time I was like the dear God himself, for in my mind arose a marvelous sky, more beautiful than the great heavens which in His long dream He stretches about Him. And the moon rose in my sky like the moon in the heaven of the dear God, only larger, clearer, like a wide-open eye that looked into my heart and read my dream. And the trees stood perfectly calm and still, like the trees of the Creator, sleeping, as it were, as my trouble slept within me. — Ah well, this is mere sentiment, dear Lady; and a man should avoid sentiment in this world, lest that cross down in

the corner of his hand — on the *Mons Lunœ* as
we call it — wax too deep, and then — I told you
once the result.

As for my verses, I have put them in a form
never used before, so far as I know. It is fitting
that she who has brought new beauty into the
world, should receive her homage of praise also
in a new form.

Upward the full moon floats into the night,
    With glory greater than of things on earth;
And on the forest falls a wondrous light,
    Smiling upon the leaves in tranquil mirth.

She hovers where the long road through the woods
    Climbs to the sky from yonder sloping hill;
And down this avenue her splendor floods,
    Like as a river flowing swift and still.

The silences profound fill me with fear;
    In all this world of light I tread alone,
Save that the river, rolling past me here,
    Is parted by my shadow backward thrown;

Save o'er my thoughts a Lady of sweet pleasance,
Like yonder orient moon, her silver presence
    Lifts in my night with glory all her own.

VIII.

There is an ancient Hebrew legend to the following effect. In the early days when Adam dwelt alone in Paradise, there was no distinction of seasons, but endless summer. There was no seedtime nor harvest, but every tree and herb had on it together the green fruit and the ripe, bearing incessantly, yet without beauty or display. Flowers there were none, for the fruit appeared like the leaves without any pomp of heraldry. But when woman was created, a sudden change came over the earth. The great joy, no doubt, which the world felt at the appearance of its new mistress, gathered into that portion of the year when she was fashioned all the beauty of the months ; and always thereafter this period called spring was marked with extraordinary gladness, while the remaining seasons were left more barren and sombre. For the first time, also, flowers burst forth on every side, to reappear with the dawn of each succeeding year. They were the signal of supreme joy in the world's heart, as well might be. — This is only a flimsy legend to be sure ; but we are prone to seek remote reasons for our actions, and this may afford a pretty explanation of the pleasure a man takes in sending flowers to a woman. They bloomed for you, it is said, and belong to you quite naturally. And so —

If roses might in thee awake
  The joy thou giv'st my heart,
Then earth would dare have flowers as fair
  As thou, their regent, art.

Yet hold them to thy brow, my Queen!
  And it will be the gale
In balmy weather hath blown together
  Roses and lilies pale.

Or lift them to thy lips, my Queen!
  And though I walk in night,
Within my heart a joy will start,
  A planet of delight.

Yet lay them on thy breast, my Queen!
  And if they wither there,
Then wilt thou learn what fires may burn
  'Twixt rapture and despair?

IX.

I fear the poem you will find enclosed is
somewhat irrelevant. Indeed I came to my
desk intending to write down quite other words,
more to the point, perhaps, but too presumptuous
to proceed from one who styles himself only a
servant. In some way to restrain myself from
writing what might have brought me bitter repentance, I indited the following lines which had

been composed some time since. They are in character. Istar, you know, was the old Semitic goddess of beauty and love, very desirable for the eyes, whose breath was so sweet that beneath it the flowers unfolded, and whose influence was so strong that the tides rose under her feet. Certain forward scholars claim that her name is merely another form of the Persian Esther, which itself means a star, and might well be given to one whose glory has ever been symbolized to the people by the white planet of evening. However that may be, fancy a young man, grown weary of living in the long reveries of the monks, and dejected by the tumult of ambitions, who unexpectedly becomes acquainted with the legend of this pagan divinity, with this goddess whose beauty seemed so passionate and unregretful, that the soul which had but once looked upon her unveiled brow would bear with it something of her joy and whiteness even into the darkness of death. Such a man might have written what you will now peruse.

Istar, at whose sweet-falling breath the flower
   Unfoldeth on the bough its dainty art,
For whom the tides in elemental power
   Heave with the beating of a human heart;

Unveil to me thy brow's whole loveliness,
   And Jesus' bloody sweat and dropping tears,

I will deny, with all that men confess —
The builded hope of two long thousand years.

But let thy maid unveil to me thine eyes,
    And all the high ambitions of our race,
The proud achievements and the power they
        prize,
    I will renounce, and bear me in disgrace.

O Istar, lady of the fragrant breath,
Let not my soul go the long way of death,
    Unwhitened by the glory of thy face !

X.

I have been meditating religious subjects all this
evening, and am now in so exalted a state of piety
that I can not refrain from writing you one of
those sermons which I have so often threatened.
For many months now, I have been buried in the
dusty tomes of the mediæval clerks. Often you
wonder what I find so absorbing in these almost
forgotten writers ; perhaps my sermon may explain the mystery to you. Certainly this world
of monkish musings will be to me still more fas-
cinating if your sympathy can follow me into its
obscure haunts. Accordingly, my text is not found
in the Bible, but is a sentence from one of the
earliest of the schoolmen, John Scotus Erigena,
a mystic, a pantheist, and something of a heretic ;

but this last character does not preclude the pious
use to which I would put him. They tell me
that last Sunday the Reverend —— preached on
the divine purpose of Satan, that arch-heretic
himself; and shall not we, then, find profit in the
musings of so mild a sinner as aerial Erigena?
This particular sentence of our mystic has been
tormenting me (you know how an unusual expression, or strain of music may cling to one)
ever since I read it, several weeks ago, so that it
has driven more sober reflections quite out of my
mind, and I have even caught myself mumbling
the words aloud in inopportune places.—But
you must be impatient for the text:—

"Nam qui amat vel deligit, ipse patitur:
    qui vero amatur vel deligitur, agit."

And now that it is written, I feel almost as if
my sermon were delivered; and as if any explanation added would only detract from the force
of these strange words: "For he who desires or
loves, is indeed acted upon: but he who is desired or loved, acts!"

They occur without much apparent connection
in the midst of a long and, I suppose, tedious
dissertation on the nature and attributes of God.
In God, he saith, all contraries meet and all im-
perfections are completed: for He is the supreme
affirmation who creates and is not created, and
again, the supreme negation who neither creates
nor is created. He is the absolute quiet resulting

from all conflicting motions, the attainment of
all desires in whom is nothing to be desired; so
that in Him motion is rest and rest is motion, to
desire is to be satisfied, and to be satisfied is to
desire.   It is in this connection, to show linguist-
ically how passive verbs may in sense be active,
and *vice versâ*, that our text is introduced.   And
yet it is brought in abruptly, irrelevantly, and
quite without comment, so that when I came to
it in the course of my reading, I had to go back
and gather up again the thread of the argument.
It seems as if the musty old schoolman writing
at his desk was disturbed in his meditations by
some fine object passing before him.   Perhaps
he caught, through his window, a glimpse of the
world more alluring than ordinary, a vision of the
early spring and the awakening of life ; and out
of half-forgotten memories thus rekindled of his
youthful days, wove this exquisite little lyric into
the sombre web of his argument — for it is a
lyric of singular beauty, is it not?   And of a
sudden, as I was reading, the blurred, ill-printed
quarto page of my book became, as it were, a
richly illuminated scroll, on whose margin wonderfully radiant faces were portrayed in gold
and fine colors.   The long dream of the middle
ages rose in my sight as a radiant woman step-
ping toward me out of a forest decked with
the colors of spring; and that day I read no
more.

You begin to understand the meaning of the words, do you not? *Qui amat vel diligit, ipse patitur ; qui vero amatur vel diligitur, agit.* — A very trite illustration will make them clearer. If one had not been told otherwise, he might infer that the humming of an Æolian harp was caused by some mechanism curiously contrived within the instrument ; whereas in truth this is quite passive, and the stirring of the chords is from without. So, too, if we had never seen the sun rise, might we not suppose the early dawn to spring in some way from the heart of the earth itself ? Yet we know that but for the emanations from the sun, our world would wander altogether dark and without an orbit, in the hollows of space. These comparisons are commonplace enough, but for that very reason may serve to elucidate what would seem, at first, the paradoxical caprice of an idle brain — and possibly a dangerous caprice. For Erigena was a master among those subtle pantheists to whom the whole fabric of creation was a mere phantasm, a dream of the all-embracing divinity : to whom the imaginings of the human brain were other worlds within the great world of God, as real as this but more limited ; so that truth became to them the mere following of the perilous ways of the fancy : to whom, if we follow the guiding of our text, the palpable substance of a fair human form was not so real a thing as the indwelling

power or personality of Beauty itself, the *vis pul-
chritudinis ipsius,* as Erigena calls it, which
might in some wise emanate from its abode as an
ethereal spirit or individuality, and render whomsoever it chose subject to its influence. This, indeed, is the very essence of mediæval realism,
and consequently of pantheism, that beauty is
more intensely real than the beautiful object,
and desire is more a living creature than the
thing desired. So it was, I fancy, that our
learned schoolman was betrayed into writing the
words of our text.

And I myself can easily conceive how a man
might feel a new passion arise within him, so different from the usual tenor of his sensations that
he would be brought to apply thereto some mystical interpretation like this of Erigena; not presuming to suppose so fair a disposition was born
of himself, but rather that he was the passive instrument touched by a spiritual emanation from
without. So doubtless the word passion itself
came to be used, from *passus est.* And further
I can conceive that a peculiar kind of fear might
awake in him, lest this feeling or passion which
appeared so salutary, yet in another sense so
foreign, to his heart, might pass away from him,
being, as he judged, not in his own control but
in the power of another. His love would seem
to him only the garnering of that light which at
the will of another might cease utterly to shine

upon him; *nam qui amat, ipse patitur; quæ vero amatur, agit.*

This is my sermon; and you must admit, as the great Chalmers used to say when pressed on the merits of a poor preacher: " Ah, but his text was fine! " And finally, we ministers of the Word always claim that the moral of our discourse lies with the hearer. So be it, and *missa est.*

XI.

To my Lady in Washington, greeting. — Last night, as I wrote you, I was at my friend A.'s in the whirl of festivities. The air was mild with the flavor of returning spring, and early in the evening I slipped out of the parlors unobserved to refresh myself in the garden. The contrast after the harassing bustle within doors was soothing and grateful. Already the grass was soft and yielding to the foot, a light breeze stirred the leafless shrubs; below me the winding Riverside Drive lay like a silver stream of water, and beyond the terrace the real river was gliding " at his own sweet will," beautiful and mysterious in the starry light. Over the Jersey hills the new moon was setting behind the trees, sharp and bent like a scimitar, having the peculiar dull orange hue of heated steel when first losing its lustre. As the trees beneath it swayed in the wind, it seemed to take their motion, as if it were, forsooth, a sabre brandished in the heavens. Not far above it and on a line passing midway between the upturned horns of the moon, hung Venus, lustrous and white beyond her wont, her pure radiance contrasting sharply with the ruddy color of the other. The old surprise overcame me at this wondrous spectacle, and the same unanswered question rose to my lips. What delusion works in the sky that so much splendor passes with no meaning or oracular message to mankind? What perversity has willed that forebodings of death should abide in the same soul with the perception of so supreme a glory? And then a second thought followed quickly. What doth my absent Lady Queen at this moment? Would that she too were touched by this same splendor! But immediately conscience smote me, saying: "Would the wise Governor of the starry orbits arrange so much beauty in the heavens for thy delight only, and that Lady not behold the glory of her own!" Surely some spirit must dwell in thee, kindred to the light of those worlds above, and I think more than once I have detected such in thine eyes and in the radiance of thy brow. And whenever the stars set themselves in a chorus of peculiar grace, of a truth some secret influence descends into thy breast, speaking with thee, so that, wheresoever thou art and howsoever occupied, the sympathetic voice calls thee out into the night to behold and enjoy the glory that is

thine own. You will laugh at this vagary of
mine, but tell me, is there not some truth in it?

The whole city mourns until you return, fair
Lady.

XII.

You have never, I suppose, read the Latin
works of Giordano Bruno. They are in I do
not know how many volumes; and the language
which the heretic deigns to use is arid, exceedingly crooked, and at times quite untranslatable.
Indeed, they would not attract any one whose
mind was not equally arid, crooked, and perhaps
untranslatable, like themselves. There is something disdainful in his manner of writing, too;
as if he who could say that it did not repent him
to have undergone labors and tribulation and exile for the truth's sake, because in brief labor he
found long rest, in slight pain immense joy, and
in narrow exile the amplest fatherland — as if
such an one would purposely leave something of
the labor and separation in his written words to
warn off the indifferent and feeble, and if possible make the truth when found more precious
and sweet. For his words do proclaim the truth,
the mightiest truth all these centuries of investi-
gation have discovered.

Perhaps also some foreboding of his struggle
with the church and of his martyrdom at the
stake prompted him to involve his more daring

heresies in intricate obscurity. His works, like St. Paul's, are sometimes hard to understand. But this afternoon I was reading in his " De Immenso et Innumerabilibus," and found one passage which I am sure will interest you.

Bruno lived, you know, in a peculiar age, when the internecine war between religion and science was at its height. Copernicus had published his great blasphemy that the earth revolves about the sun. It seemed to the religious that faith must pass away if this heresy went unchallenged. For they said, and wisely, if our world is only an insignificant point in the heavens, only a subordinate member of a system which is itself but one among innumerable systems that sweep through the immensity of space, — why then, who will believe that Providence orders this infinite universe for the profit of men, that the sun and stars change their courses for our benefit, that the ruler of all these moving worlds dwelt for a time within the limits of human frailty? Our heretic gave up everything and became a wanderer and an exile in all lands in order to proclaim this new doctrine of the infinity of space, and of the position of our globe in the star-strewn ways of the universe. There is something heroic, is there not, in the thought of this man, persecuted and reviled, traveling from city to city, confronting all men with this strange new belief, and finally burning at the stake. I know of but one

parallel in history, Xenophanes of old, before the
days of Socrates, who wandered solitary among
the cities of Hellas, preaching before the light-
hearted Greeks his solemn message concerning
the One God.⁻ I can see now the aged minstrel
chanting to the lyre his mystic song ; the inspiration of his mien awes the multitude, but they
smile when his numbers tell them the gods of
Homer and Hesiod are a lie, that the divinities
of Olympus are empty names, that there is One
God, infinite, eternal, invisible, without shadow
of change, who is all-beholding, all-knowing, all-
hearing.

The mission of Bruno was not far different
from this, for he too had this vision of the infinite
to utter. It seems strange to us that science
should have been the votary of romance in those
days ; but the age and doctrine of our heretic
were remarkable in this, that wonder made the
new science a religion. Weird spectres from
the past ages of faith haunted the new world of
inquiry, and made the paths of thought perilous.
Something in Bruno's belief reminds one of the
most beautiful moment of modern positivism.
I mean that sort of scientific pantheism which
recognizes life in all things as a fragment of the
universal force underlying every movement and
change. Only in Bruno this doctrine was a purer
and more poetical intuition, which suffered his
spirit to commune with the macrocosmic spirit, to

be rapt away into it and become a part, nay even
the very reality, of this world-soul. He opens the
long poem I mentioned with some such mystical
revery as this : That there is a mind or soul
which has inspired his breast with a new sense,
such a sense as makes the wings to expand on
birds, and which has lifted his heart to seek a lofty
goal. By the inspiration of this spirit we despise
fortune and death ; the secret gates are opened
and the chains are sundered whence but few have
escaped. Centuries, years, months, days, the
numerous progeny and arms of Time, to which
not even brass or adamant are hard, have passed
him by untouched in their fury. Intrepidly his
mind rises through the illimitable ether. The
.crystal spheres and the dark vapors give way before him, and that feigned adamantine rampart
of the universe. And ever as he soars upward past
the innumerable swift-wheeling worlds, his soul is
filled with the sublimity of endless life. He is
Leader, Law, Light, Prophet, Father, Creator, and
the great Journey itself. — This is bold language
for the sixteenth century, is it not? The words
may mean to convey only the exalted enthusiasm that stirs the mind on first casting off the
restraints of the feigned *flammantia moenia
mundi* and realizing the conception of infinite
space ; but I think beyond this they tell the
old, old secret that has haunted man from the
beginning, the mysterious lore of the East,

glimpses of which come to me in the silence of
night but leave me with the returning dawn.
Some day I shall hold fast the elusive visitant
and write you its name.

But it is another part of Bruno's belief concerning which I wished especially to write you.
When he endeavored to account for the newly
discovered revolutions of the planets, his poetical,
one might say religious, inspiration did not forsake
him.   Newton had not yet worked out the law of
gravitation : and to Bruno this wonderful circling
of the stars in their orbits was not the result of
delicately balanced forces, beautiful in their opera-
tion yet quite dead and mechanical; but in each
planet dwelt a living emanation of the Deity,
a soul full of the joy of untrammeled power,
and, like the blessed in Dante's Paradiso, forever spinning about in the ecstasy of delight.
To him, as to the older philosophers, the circle
was symbolical of perfect harmony ; and so these
planet-souls wheeled in swift, unceasing circles
about their source, for any other motion had
been unworthy of them.   And there seemed to be
some sort of worship in their unsleeping attend-
ance on the sun in his larger journey through space,
as if gratitude impelled them for the sweet light
which he so plentifully poured upon them.   Some
notion of the Pythagorean harmony of the spheres
was also in Bruno's mind, the planets calling one
to another through the vast expanse when their

crossing orbits brought them nearer together, calling to one another expressions of good will for one brief moment and then plunging again into the solitudes of darkness. This sounds fantastical to us now; but after all, when we have changed a few words, does it not mean much the same thing as our own grayer explanation of the phenomena? It seemed so to me this evening when I saw Jupiter walking in the mid-heaven; and it occurred to me that the old mystic may have come quite as near the truth as we, and in how beautiful a manner!—for it is beautiful, this subtle pantheism of the poets, as if all things were alive and but members of the one God whose pleasure is displayed in the glory of women and the whiteness of the planets.

You, too, have been named a star, Lady Esther. And to me, who am not comely as you are, but turbid within and quite plain without, to me has been given, perhaps as a sort of compensation, one faculty not altogether commonplace — I mean the insatiable desire to know the beautiful things of this world, to trace them through hidden resemblances in difficult and remote regions. It may be my power stops here, and I am unable to lead others where I have been. And yet when I meet any rare fancy like this of Bruno's, my first impulse is to repeat it to you: for it seems to me I can choose no higher lot than to employ my god-given powers in rendering your pathway through life still more wondrously fair. And if next time you regard the stars these words of a dreamer in Gotham give you a moment's pleasure or add new meaning to the beauty of their motion, I shall not repent having puzzled over these pages of crooked Latin, or having run the risk of annoying you with what may be only a tedious homily, or even something far more hazardous.

The following translation of Leopardi's " L' Infinito " may give substance to my own vague musings.

Ever to me this unfrequented slope
   Was dear, this garden-closure that around
Cuts off the far horizon with its cope.
   And sitting, gazing thus, — beyond that bound
Unmeasured spaces, silences sublime
   I fashion in my thought, and quietude
Surpassing human ways : there for a time
   My heart no longer fears. And while the rude
Wind murmurs in the branches, I anon
   That infinite silence with this voice compare :
And I remember the eternal one,
   The seasons of the dead, and this of care
About us and its sound. So as I wonder
My thought in this immensity sinks under ;
   And shipwreck in that sea is sweet to bear.

XIII.

You will not think me, Lady Esther, fallen into one of those moods of the imagination which you so relentlessly accuse of untrustworthiness, if I write very simply and very frankly that you were more beautiful to-night than I have ever before seen you. I am sure I cannot say what was the reason of this. Perhaps the thread of beads about your throat had something to do with it, as they glimmered like so many drops of dew on the chalice of a lily, or better yet — but I fear to incur your displeasure. Perhaps it was my own infatuated eyes, and you are always just as radiantly fair — as indeed I believe is the truth. Certainly I was a little disturbed by your appearance. With this living light in my eyes it is natural that I failed utterly to appreciate your collection of photographic views, though I could see your displeasure at my indifference; and this is one reason why I write now as I do. For it occurred to me in your presence last night as never before, that here after all, almost within reach of my breath, is that very strange something we call beauty, that elusive harmony of form which must have troubled the vision of Scopas when he carved the Roman statue; which was on the face of Beatrice, so that Dante was moved to say he would write of her such things as had never been dreamed, so that by the mere looking into her eyes he was upborne from planet to planet; which the young Raphael discerned on the brow of a living woman, so that henceforth his art and religion could lift him no higher than the endeavor to multiply one ideal face for man's eternal consolation.

I might easily add other examples, but I have said enough to explain my lack of enthusiasm while looking over the pictures; for in the end these efforts of art must appear quite tame, must they not, when brought face to face with what at least seems to us their living ideal and prototype. Philosophers have written many books to explain to us, if possible, the nature of the union of spirit and matter, the wedding of the eternal and the finite. Plotinus, if I remember rightly, using Aristotelian terms, calls form in matter the domination of spirit over the inert *hyle;* and says that just so far as form predominates does the spiritual become manifest; so that harmony of form, or beauty, is for our eyes the symbol of the eternal God dwelling in the world. The saints who dwell among us from time to time, strive by the purity of their lives to proclaim this same indwelling of divinity within mortal things. But the poets and artists, the beloved children of Apollo, have ever seen this mystic union symbolized in the perfect face of some woman, whether seen in the actual world or beheld at rare times passing majestically through the shadowy cham-

bers of their soul. And I think even the build-
ers of the great cathedrals were impelled to
their task by the same vision which haunted those
who painted the radiant madonnas to live on
their walls. Some form of this sort must have
appeared to the ancient Gothic architect, as in
the dusk of evening he walked under the trees,
whose branches met in pointed arches over his
head. The level rays of the setting sun poured
through the interlacing boughs like the crimson
and purple light of a rose-window, when evening sets it aflame. And before him in the
deeper twilight floated the face of the wonderful
madonna, forever eluding him in the changing
shadows. So it was he saw the plan of that
great building he was to erect to Our Lady —
Notre Dame.

Perhaps it was something like this — the fair
face I mean — that I thought I saw last night,
and that troubled the depths of my being until
I may have become even a little petulant, as Poe
would call it, under the stress of desire. And
on the long way home, crossing the silent bay,
the recollection of what things others had been
led to accomplish by such a vision still haunted
me. It seemed to me that this loveliness of form
and spirit was too high for me alone, or for any
other individual, to see and possess in his imagination ; and a longing was born to speak of it in
the ears of all men, that this feeling toward you

might become a part of the universal admiration and love of mankind for beauty. But then the old doubts came back, of my weakness and distrust and ignorance, of my own unworthiness, and of man's nature mated with all the base things of creation. For he who shall bring new perception of beauty to men must have his own mortal vision purged of the doubts of this blinder age, which would find nothing divine in man but only a more perfect animal. You remember the story of the Athenian, how he killed the Minotaur, half man and half bull, in the intricate labyrinth whence no adventurer had ever escaped. Last night this legend came to me as symbolical of the struggle now waging within some of us. And thus, I thought, —

I wander in a labyrinth of doubt,
    Of ways innumerable with error filled,
Whose troubled windings know no passage out, —
    A blind abode no righteous art would build.

And in the centre dwells that monstrous birth,
    The shame of Crete, as if our human pride
Were mated to the vulgar things of earth,
    And all our nobler hope and faith denied.

Yet in my hand love's slender thread I hold,
    Whose guiding may retrace the perilous path ;
And this sweet confidence hath made me bold
    To brave the error and the monster's wrath.

Dear Princess, here without thy inspiration,
My heart were lost indeed in desolation,
   And in thy love resides all hope it hath.

XIV.

. . . Repentance hath kept me up till long
after all good Christians should be in bed. As a
token of my anxious vigil, I send the verses you
will find within. You may take them for a con-
tinuation of what I was saying in my last note.
I am not sure they have any poetic value, but for
their sincerity I will vouch with my head.

INCOGNITO.

There is a Valley-land where mortal doubts
   Beneath the boughs of sorrow prowl at large,
Or chase our nobler things in brawling routs
   Along the shadow of the forest-marge.

There Death and menial Cares and sullen Scorn
   Hold the World-Beauty as a captive queen;
There waste the Virgins of Delight, forlorn,
   In dungeons where no dawn is ever seen.

Thither I journey as an errant knight,
   Wearing his Princess' scarf for fealty,
And pledged, until his rusted arms are bright
   With many a dint, his only peace to flee.

Dear Princess! in thy bosom bear my name;
For some return with laurels of sweet fame,
    While some — nay, love is more than victory.

XV.

DE PROFUNDIS.

I tossed her flower in the snow,
For with so chary grace 't was given me,
Colder it scarce could be
Where winds of winter bitterly drift and blow.
So under the high-suspended city light
Where every eye may see,
There may it rest in the snow,
A drop of blood upon the frozen white.
And yet — ah well, I know,
I know not whether was colder all that night
My heart or the flower in the snow!

XVI.

The sun set over the bay this evening more
splendid than usual.   Surely you must have seen
it all, the light in the heavens and the mighty
host of clouds swimming in the tide, for the illumination striking your western windows must
have allured you from any duty.   It seemed to
me I had never beheld so pure and radiant a yellow, the color of the flowers of sulphur, suffused
over the western horizon in so spotless a band.

A little above floated a shoal of broken clouds whose lower border lay quite parallel with the black line of the earth. They were of all tints of red, and all supremely beautiful; the crimson hue predominated, forming a fine contrast with the yellow band below. On some of them I could detect a delicate white edge like a thread of burnished silver. Most wonderful of all was the evening star, Venus, whose brilliance we have remarked so often of late. To-night she hung in the very middle of the glowing yellow sunlight, between the clouds and our horizon line. Strange as it may sound, her dazzling whiteness was only intensified by the sea of splendor from which she beamed; as a diamond, I always think, sparkles most nobly from the bosom of a fair woman.

I stood gazing intently at the spectacle till all its loveliness had faded away, and the new glories of the stars began to assemble overhead, passing the light from one to another as in the torch races of ancient Greece. And as I watched, a vision of the old pantheist Erigena stole into my meditation, and the fading sunlight and the burning clouds took on a new and spiritual significance. From the window of his cell, or from a westward slope of his convent garden, some such evening scene as this must surely have flashed upon his tired eyes at the end of his long labor, and inspired the closing chapters of his work "Concerning Nature." Truly our God dwelleth in unapproachable light, and clouds are the curtains of his throne. And this is not a symbol peculiar to one man or one religion, but is the natural language of adoration among all peoples. The unfathomable splendor of light, filling the dome of the heavens from horizon to horizon, is ever symbolical of the infinite Wisdom dwelling afar off above created things, one and universal, embracing the whole world. And the clouds — have you ever considered that, of all the phenomena among which we dwell, they alone suffer perpetual change ? The mountains, the valleys, and the level plains are ever the same save for the slight variations of herbage and leaves, and even this diversity follows the regular period of the seasons. The seas, but for the painted canopy that overhangs them, would have only one hue ; and the waves that rise and subside vary in magnitude alone. The broad rivers and the tiny streams are forever moving, yet know no alteration. How different are the clouds! The purple bands of dawn, the snowy mountains or the light fleece of noon, the panorama of evening! The storm-clouds, black or livid or green ; the leaden cloak of winter and the white vesture of summer! There is endless mutation without system or order. Such a fluttering curtain is drawn before the steadfast firmament, of all created things the symbol of stability and duration, which knows but one change, the unvarying alternation of day and night. Surely this unfathomable sky is the very government of the world, involving in mysterious immutability the mutations of light and darkness, of pleasure and pain, of goodness and evil: and the clouds that sweep thereunder, veiling it from our eyes yet reflecting its glory, are the world of illusion, the shifting appearance of things that holds our understanding in servile subjection.

And now I comprehended why my old master, the monkish enthusiast, desired in his contemplation to be rapt into the clouds, nay rather to ascend above their heights into the unveiled vision of the empyrean. And as the clouds, moving below the serenity of heaven, are made iridescent by its white light and glow with a myriad variegated hues, so the visible world of creation and the intelligible spheres of our thought were to this mystic full of the meaning of God: theophanies in which the ineffable glory of the Unseen became perceptible to man. For this reason the Son of Man is said always to come with the clouds; as Daniel beheld him in the night-visions approaching the Ancient of Days, meaning thereby that thus is revealed to us the Infinite incarnate in material forms. So also we whose vision is strong to discern the face of God in his works, shall be lifted up into the purer contemplation of Himself — *rapiemur in nubibus obviam Christo in aera, et sic semper cum illo erimus —*

for we shall be like Christ, being ourselves incar-
nations of the living light. — Did the visionary
mystic mean even more ?

And in the end I wonder what were your
meditations, if you too saw this marvelous sunset.
Indeed you protest that these fancies of mine are
foreign to your thought. The beauty of the sky
fills you often with beatific peace, but without the
symbolic meanings which ever haunt my mind.
And I believe you ; for this manner of refracting
beauty into curious emblems and sensations must
be altogether foreign to one who dwells nearer
than my spirit can follow to the unapproachable
heavens. Thou art that star of Venus which I
beheld in the pure light midway between the
clouds and the rampart of earth, a fair white
lustre contrasted with the burning vapors of our
world. Nay,

> "Dear Child! Dear Girl!
> If thou appear'st untouched by solemn thought,
> Thy nature is not therefore less divine :
> Thou liest in Abraham's bosom all the year ;
> And worship'st at the Temple's inner shrine,
> God being with thee when we know it not."

XVII.

> The fire light glinting on her face
> Made her a fairy thing,

Upon whose forehead I could trace
All my imagining.

The shadow and the wandering light
Troubled her open eyes,
Like pools beneath the falling night
When the red sunset dies.

So in her heart unreal desires
Unbidden come and go,
Mere shadows of the burning fires
That in my bosom glow.

I remember we boys had a superstition that if we could save a sufficient quantity of peach-stones, the druggist would buy them of us and from a great heap of bruised kernels extract a drop or two of the bitter cyanic acid. Possibly the legend lingers with the youngsters of to-day, and they still devour the fruit with a mysterious sense of that awful acid within its seed.

So, sweet Princess, it may be your court-poet, like the fabled druggist, in the morning extracts from the innumerable minutes of his long night a few words of bitterness, which he sends to the queen of his days and nights — sure, not to poison her, but as the weaker essence of almonds, merely to flavor her morning curds.

Woe is me, for the end of our masquerading is come! Too well I have known from the beginning that I could touch your imagination but not your heart. It is the heavy penalty I must pay in that I myself have looked out upon the rest of the world as upon figures moving through a dream, scorning to feel for them in my heart — alas, a penalty too heavy, for my punishment is greater than my sin. And last night when the witchery of the fluttering firelight and the spell of ghostly tales had roused you into a state of exaltation, too well I knew what it signified. Madman that I was, I tore away the veil; and now what manner of man must I appear henceforth before you? I must even begin once more to weave the web of fancy about us, lest the reality of my passion terrify you indeed, and I be denied the narrow liberty that still remains.

XVIII.

Be good enough to accept herewith my banquet meditations. I am aware that I run some risk in sending them, as they may lead you to infer I was not quite sober at the time. . . . And while others listened to speeches not too brilliant, your humble servant was indulging in these jovial meditations, which he secretly indited on the back of his menu card and so carried to his home. And the fair recipient must be pleased not to smile when she reads these doleful rhymes crowded, like *entremets*, between substantial titles of flesh and fowl.

COMPENSATION.

In heaven was truce : God and the ancient Foe,
  Like stern duumvirs of the Roman state,
In secret council viewed our world of woe,
  And portioned equally the coming fate.

For every lily that the God might plant,
  Satan should rear the deadly mandragore ;
For every lark that piped his morning chant,
  Beneath the stars some nightingale deplore.

And where one human heart along his path
  Found comfort in beholding the sweet light,
His comrade on the way should see but wrath,
  And haste his journey as in hopeless flight.

So is it well, a kind of nobler duty,
If men may see unclouded all thy beauty,
  That I should walk in unillumined night.

XIX.

I do not know why I send this melancholy
poem. I have no reason to suppose you may not
be altogether weary of my dirges ; and this one
is even more lugubrious than usual. Take it for
an actual incident, if you choose, or, better yet,
as the mere fantasy of a dreamer who would give
to his moral experience the color of a dramatic
happening. —

The books have come, and I have begun my study of Sanskrit. Fain am I to see if those ancient eastern dreamers and pantheists found, in their contemplation of the deceitful Mâyâ and ineffable Brahma, that peace of heart which we of the west so vainly seek. The thought of the long and, I fear, hopeless journey I am to go in these oriental lands oppresses me; and yet dim premonitions are present of a marvelous empire of peace afar off, I know not where, toward the rising of the sun. Many books I must read, bewilder my brain with uncouth languages; but some day shall I not return like a voyager of old, after traversing distant seas; and, kneeling at the feet of the Princess whose flag I have borne so far, shall I not implore as a recompense for long exile, that I may kiss the royal hand which receives from me a new and glorious empire in .the east?

THE LOST PRAYER.

At night once pausing in the outer hall,
    A woman's prayer he heard of weary breath: —
" Forgive, O Lord, his doubting lest he fall,
    And I should lose him in the world of death!"

Methought among the shadows of the night
    He saw that prayer go forth; and saw it roam
Like a lost child, forwearied by affright,
    Who wanders in the dark and wails for home.

In the unfathomable ways above,
  Where the great worlds unceasingly are tost,
" Forgive, O Lord," he heard its cry of love,
  " The world of death ! " — then in the void
    't was lost.

And he, the listener, filled with strange foreboding,
Turned also to the night, and wandered brooding
  Till all the stars their lonely way had crossed.

XX.

. . . But the distractions of the day, like
all other mortal things, have passed into "the
backward and abysm of time ; " and I am in my
own room, where my books are, and a fine silver
penholder is in my hand — a dainty silver trinket
with sober motto graven thereon : " *Eheu ! fu-
gaces labuntur anni,*" — and I would to God I
might get those words out of my mind ! You
know why I prize this toy above all my other
possessions. But beyond this value of associa-
tion, the solemn words of its admonition have
sunken deep into my heart, and make it, as it
were, a mentor of my daily work. Can I write
anything trivial or base or ephemeral, with this
warning in my hand, this warning of that same
" backward and abysm of time " as Master Will
styles it. That is a sort of madness of mine, — a
lunacy, or what shall I call it ? — never to have

this feeling of runaway time out of my mind, and
never quite to forget the miserable end, when
days and months and years, for me at least, shall
be mingled and indistinct — lost like the little
down-hill streams in a sea that is much too big
for them.   So time shall end.

Another consummation is prophesied in the
Apocalypse, I know.   For an angel shall stand
with one foot on sea and one foot on land, and
shall swear by the Everlasting *quia tempus non
erit amplius.*   This is not death, perhaps, but
that swallowing up of Time in Eternity, that
word of the *Regnant Now*, which is to the verita-
ble seer the purpose of all true philosophy, even
here in this world of sequence.   It may be such
wisdom as this shall be given to me also in the
end, but now, —

"Knowledge comes, but wisdom lingers; and I linger on
      the shore,
And the individual withers, and the world is more and
      more."

But this other cessation of time, which we call
death, and which comes to sage and fool alike,
woe unto him who hears the wings of this Angel
ever beating in the silent air of night; who distinguishes the footsteps of this Messenger among
the sounds of the thoroughfare by day.   For him
the present is lost, yet the peace of eternity is not
fulfilled.   Pray you, Lady Esther, know you no
sweet medicament, no healing balm for so sad a

malady, no charm to allure a doting brain from the dark and vasty backward and forward of time into the safer Now?   Often when the poor luna-tic, of whom we speak, is sitting with you and trying to communicate with you, he thinks that all his wandering in the dreary kingdom of Time is just to learn some new and worthier speech in which to utter your beauty — and then he essays to sing, only to find he is moonstruck after all and nothing more.   Pray God for me his mad-ness may have just a spark of that divine mania which Plato described of old as the inspiration of the gods. — And all this for my pen!

XXI.

A very pretty edition of "The Imitation of Christ" has come into my possession, and I have just read the book through again for the first time in many months.   You must be familiar with the work, and can imagine how deeply it impressed me.   However different in profession, yet in spirit how much it resembles the "Medita-tions" of Marcus Aurelius and other stoics, how much, too, Spinoza and the later pantheists. There is but one truth for them all, that the things of this world are delusive, vain, transi-tory, mere shadows and fluctuating symbols of the Eternal which they hide rather than reveal. I think the old Hebrew Ecclesiastes said it better

than all who have succeeded him — *Vanitas vani-
tatum!* — And they each and all can find but
one remedy; atheist and Christian alike cry out
that we must give up father and mother, brother
and sister, all the ties and endearments of life,
love and friendship, all the pleasures and pursuits of the world — all these we must surrender,
and for what? To the pagan that his individual
life may be absorbed into the universal stream,
flowing blindly or intelligently he knows not, to
what end he knows not, wherein the peculiar desires of his soul must be swallowed up as a wave
is lost in the general current. This is the philosopher's life of contemplation.

The Christian finds no gentler remedy, only
his universe assumes a ruler and personal chief
whom he calls God. To be sure à Kempis
speaks of a better life to follow, and has a passion of love for that god-man Jesus who repre-
sents to him the mystic wedding of the finite and
the infinite, of his own individuality with the universal being. Yet at what expense is this hope
and communion purchased? I think nothing
more terrible was ever written than this cry, to
me the essence of the whole Imitation: "But
woe be to them that know not their own misery;
and a greater woe to them that love this miserable and corruptible life!" And this is the cry
of the soul who has found God, who strives to
imitate the Creator of life. It is comparable to

the *pensée* of Pascal : " The grandeur of man lies
in this, that he knows himself miserable." It is
said, too, that Saint Theresa, who sums up in
herself so much of the aspiration and triumph of
medieval religion, used often to ejaculate in her
prayers, " *Domine, aut mori aut pati !* " and the
refrain of one her most passionate songs is burdened with the same cry : " *Morior quia non morior !* " Indeed, the whole life of the Seraphic
Virgin is but the repetition of this moral, that
only in the utter abnegation of the joys of this
life can the peace of eternity be found. As a
young woman her greatest sorrow was that she
could not shed tears when reading the passion
of the Lord. She tells in her autobiography
how the perusal of a certain work on prayer
taught her to collect her mind more ardently on
heavenly things. So she adds simply : " *Lacry-
marum donum jam a Domino acceperam, atque
ipsa lectione multum recreabar.*" Wonderful
mystery of joy ! strange visitation of peace ! In
tears she finds the delight whereafter her spirit
yearns. And we who walk in the shadow of
doubt, we know not which is the sadder and
which is the wiser, the fortitude and disdain of
of the stoic who contemns pleasure and pain
alike, or the anguish and humiliation of the
monk who deliberately loses his life to gain life.

Between the two lies the world of the indifferent, and, I begin to surmise, the world of the

artist who in his own way would likewise escape from the trammels of earthly things. Reject me not as indifferent or shallow if I tell you that peace, if it come at all, must find me also in this last manner. Nay, if you knew with what tumultuous strivings I have striven to find this *summam requiem*, this God, be it of Christian or philosopher, that I might so much as hear the sound of his voice afar off, or but touch the hem of his garment, like the woman who touched Jesus and was healed — if you knew all this, surely I should have your sympathy for that distraction of manner which so often seems to withdraw me even from the charmed circle of your influence. And if, by way of apology for these moments of abstraction, I send you a handful of ill-contrived verses, remember always what deep longings impel me toward the world of art. But enough of this for the present, fair Esther, star among women. Let me tell you a vision. Last night as I lay in bed, I looked out of the window at my side. A great tree quite shut in my view, but through the gently swaying branches I could now and again catch glimpses of the sky beyond, which seemed infinitely far removed in the night, and which I knew surrounded the whole earth with its impenetrable circle. This tree, I thought to myself, is an emblem of the visible world that moves before our eyes, and the deep sky concealed by it is that God whom I seek. And even as I said this to myself, a great limb bowed down as if bent by the weight of an invisible hand, and through the aperture I beheld for a moment a wonderful white star palpitating alone in the depths. So with a silent prayer to the new light, I closed my eyes and soon fell asleep. And now must I unriddle my vision?

XXII.

Was it Da Gama or Magellan — the latter, I think in his tragic voyage around the world — who was so alarmed by the new aspect of the sky as he sailed southward. Night after night the familiar northern constellations sank deeper into the mists of the horizon he was fleeing, and one by one were lost from view. At the same time, the southern stars rose constantly higher above him, till the great planets and the moon circled directly overhead, and new constellations of unknown appearance climbed out of the dim horizon before them. Most of all was he terrified when the Polar star, by which he had steered his course, was no longer visible; for over the south pole hung no steady light, but only a vague blurred nebula, not easily distinguishable from the vapors of the ocean. Imagine his situation: sailing on boundless unknown seas, toward lands unnamed, or mentioned only by rumor, while night after night the very stars of heaven shifted northward — it was, indeed, a new heaven and a new earth. One constellation, it is said, he greeted always with increasing delight as it mounted ever higher toward the zenith — the great Southern Cross which hung in the sky with unimaginable splendor.

The tradition may be of Da Gama or of Magellan ; both were in search of the fabled land of India, whose fame, since the days of the earliest Greek explorers, had filled the western world with awe. Out of India came silks and spices and luxurious fabrics ; out of India came the stupendous myths which had troubled the young Christian world with ineradicable heresies. Out of India, too, came legends of naked forest-dwellers whose wisdom surpassed the measure of occidental conception, wisdom which held in contempt the profit and the control of mundane laws.

Both of our explorers reached the desired land, one returning to add a new continent to the realm of his sovereign, the other leaving his body in the new ocean he had traversed. But I think either of them would have deemed it sufficient reward for his long labors to have knelt at the feet of his Queen with offerings of oriental jewels and fabrics which he had brought from so far, to have adorned her beauty with exotic lustre for courtly eyes, and to have added to her empire even a small portion of those vast regions of fable. — And it is not unlikely that many a quiet scholar in these later days starts on a similar voyage of discovery in the still more fabulous lands and seas of ancient learning; with hopes akin to those of the early navigators; through difficulties, too, not altogether despicable, and dangers to the spiritual life that only the dreamer knows. The old truths which guided him may sink away into the mists of doubt; over the new pole of his heavens may float only an uncertain nebula; and out of the southern horizon may creep strange constellations, monstrous unspeakable fancies that fill him with awe, possibly, also, the great cross, with its marvelous magnificence. And one of them, if he return safely from the fantastic dominion of dreams which the Hindu seers established so many centuries ago, will be proud to kneel before the Princess under whose flag he sails, with offerings of new similitudes and oriental legends which may extend the empire of her beauty over generations of men yet to be born — if she will but be pleased to smile on the prostrate mariner. Great things may come out of the east, dear Princess.

XXIII.

For a good many days, now, a fine woodthrush has been pouring out his matutinal and vesper songs from one of our trees. Curiosity and some intimate sympathy of feeling has led me to listen attentively to his refrain, while a hankering after knowledge of the fabulous bird-language has induced me to seek a definite meaning in his oft-repeated chant.   Since the experiments of a learned professor with monkey-talk, I am not ashamed to confess my credulity in this matter, and forsooth you will see that I have gone so far as to attempt some sort of conversation with the garrulous songster.   You will see, also, and I acknowledge it with regret, that my effort is lame enough to throw ridicule on the whole undertaking.   Yet I swear that real intelligence was conveyed to me by this bird's note, and doubt not but that larger experience would render all the music of the summer forests intelligible to us.   How I wish now that less of my time and strength had been devoted to long-forgotten human languages, and more to this subtle speech of our feathered kin.   Even the silent proclamations of the stars are plainer to me than the sounds warbled in every tree.   Study and practice, as you know, have taught me to spell the future in the lettered page of the firmament; but now that I would understand and translate for your sake the simple accents of a throstle, behold what awkwardness distracts my powers : —

Now tell me, throstle, pretty bird,
  Wherefore thy merry note?

I, too, would sing, but sudden cares
　　And sorrow stop my throat. —

" I sing because I 'm happy, Sir,
　　And if it were not so,
I 'd sing to make me happy, Sir ;
　　And that is all I know." —

Ah well, but if the lady-bird
　　Who hears thy throbbing note,
Were cold as winter, would thy song
　　Freeze not within thy throat ? —

" I 'd sing and thaw her bosom, Sir,
　　And if it were not so,
I 'd sing and thaw my sorrow, Sir ;
　　And that is all I know."

This is the nearest I could catch his replies, try as I would. He is a wise bird in such matters; and wears, as an ensign of his lore, a white breast marked with reddish heart-shaped emblems. Truly next spring I will learn more of this *Magister in Amore.*

XXIV.

No doubt you have wondered why, when I write to you on so many trivial occasions, the leaden image of Saint Joseph you lent me has not inspired me with a single thought — but here you would be wrong. I have carefully followed your directions, have suspended him head downwards by a ribbon so that day and night he is upon my breast. He has been bathed in holy water, you say, and has power accordingly to grant every request. Nay, it is not lustral water that has sanctified the little image most to my regard ; but that it has hung so near your heart, has felt the throbbing of the fairest and holiest bosom in the world, this makes it reverend in my eyes and powerful to fulfil petitions. You must readily divine what request I have sent up to the pious Father — but would it surprise you to learn that I have composed a formal prayer which I offer up to him morning and evening? It is this : —

As on my heart thy form is prest,
O Spouse of Mary ! may my quest
Find harbor in thy saintly breast.

What power was over thee to win
The love of her who knew no sin,
The love of her so pure within,

So chaste within, without so fair,
The God himself might not forbear
To reckon thee his rival there ?

O Spouse of Mary ! in thy bride
Our human hearts have deified
All fairest things that here abide, —

In her, the mother of our Lord,
Who spake in him the Living Word
Of God's sweet comfort, to afford

Unto our heavy-laden brain
The knowledge we might not attain,
That Love o'er God himself doth reign.

O Spouse of Mary ! thou wast strong
To win her love who did belong
To God alone for right or wrong : —

Yet I, I know not if thy love
With all its might could rise above
My passion and the hope thereof ;

I know not if the gathered fears,
The transports and repentant tears
Of all our race through all the years,

Wherewith thy bride is made divine,
Can more than equal love like mine !
Can more than equal love like mine !

Thou Lord of Love ! from thy great dower
Spare me the semblance of thy power
To storm this summit of Love's tower.

O Spouse of Mary ! may my quest
Find harbor in thy saintly breast,
As on my heart thy form doth rest.

Rather a solemn prayer, is it not? And yet
Saint Joseph is far away, and must be quite occupied with the blandishments of his heavenly bride.
What hope can I have of reaching his ears, when
all that I say and suffer falls unheeded on you
who are so much nearer to me. Would not the
Virgin Mary be more prompt to hearken to my
plea? Somehow the words " Mary the Mother
of God " have always had a peculiar influence
over me. I think the fathers who framed the
Christian religion had a deeper insight into
human needs than any other founders of a new
creed ; and specially this fiction of " Mary the
Mother of God " shows their penetration more
clearly than any other dogma. Perhaps there
never was a religion which did not in some way
introduce this idea of the virgin mother of a god,
but it is all the work of bunglers when compared
with the faith that made the poetry of the medieval times. This is the symbolization of our
conception of infinite power united with the
purest and tenderest of human feelings — a mystic
union symbolized in a mystic fashion, for to the
reason such a conception must be illogical in the
extreme. Behold, the Almighty, the ruler of
the stars, doth here bow down from the infinite

heavens to set the seal of love on mortal lips ; and behold, a virgin of our race doth hold in her bosom the Creator of the worlds ! And men coming to worship at this shrine bring with them all the awe and reverence due to the infinite Lord of creation, and all the love and tenderness due to a virgin mother among women. — You say I am a skeptic and have no part in such a faith. It is just because I am a skeptic that it means so much to me. I am a visionary also, a dreamer, an idealist, if you please ; and it is because I am both of these that a beautiful conception like this of the Virgin Mary is a vital part of my life. I live, not in a world of faith, but in a world of imaginations ; and the sublime enunciations of Saint Augustine or the vast dreams of Erigena may have more reality to me than to many a good member of the orthodox fold. I measure such ideas by their intrinsic beauty, and not by any meagre standard of revelation or dogma.

And what has all this to do with my prayer to Saint Joseph ? You will smile when I tell you the connection, and say, as you did last night, that I am not fitted for the realities of life — and yet it is the profoundest and realest truth of my nature, the very *haecceitas* of it, truest just because it is the most ideal, this comparison of Mary and yourself which has already been intimated. I am a monk at heart, perhaps, ensnared by the toils of skepticism ; but what Mary was to the dream-

ers through the long revery of ten centuries, the
ideal beauty around which these mystics gathered
all the hopes and desires and visions and despair
of their life — all that and something more you
have become to me.   Here I have found an emblem of eternal love making radiant a form of
mortal flesh ; for somehow I conclude that only the
indwelling of the Holy Spirit in such a tabernacle
of the body, only the presence of the Spirit of
Harmony, could lure my soul to forget its disgust
of mortal things and find peace in its estrange-
ment from God.   Here in my own way I have
found the very Mother of God.   For out of mortal woman hath proceeded a vision of glory, a
wonderful hope, a reconciliation with faith, a perception of love, which shall be forevermore the
Jehovah of my aspirations.   So the musings of the
schoolmen take on a new meaning for me.   Even
the dry, mechanical ratiocinations of D. Albertus
Magnus are full of the passion of a love letter.   I
have just read the great volume of the Doctor *de
Laudibus Beatae Mariae*, and found in it no more
than an echo of my own feelings.   Even the scho-
lastic aridity of his style was a delight to me, for
it seemed to bring the hard intellectual faculties
of the brain into the service of the imaginings of
the heart, justifying the wildest vagaries of passion.   The long enumeration of excellences, the
chapters *de dulcitudine, de pulchritudine, de sua-
veolentia,* and the rest, fasten the mind with

unyielding persistence on the glory of her *quae* "*tota pulchra dicitur.*" This is the joy of worship, that all the thoughts of the heart should resolve into praises of the Blessed Mary. Ah, I could make a long letter telling of all the schoolmen, Alanus de Insulis and a host of others, who have found the highest worship of the Creator in the praises of her who was to them the Mother of God. Therefore I come to you in my humility, and bend my petitions to you when the majesty of the Almighty dazzles my sight and fills me with fear. Not to Saint Joseph shall my constant prayers ascend, but to one who shall be all compassion. Hear me, Lady of my vows!

Can you appreciate the strength of such a dream — as you may call it — to one whose life is all a dream? It is the one great reality which makes the splendor of his visions pale before the actual beauty he discerns, which assures him he is not yet entirely severed from communion with the world of appearances. It is life to him. — But I must tire you. Indeed I am altogether unhappy since last night, and am writing somehow to express my penitence. When the faithful have sinned, they repeat over and over again their *Ave Maria*, pleading in their hearts for absolution; and it is with just this intention I weary you re-reiterating what you already know so well.

XXV.

The enclosed verses were composed during the wakeful moments of a restless night, much as a traveler repeats to himself some half-remembered rhymes over and over again with the turnings of his road. I have done this often while walking in the Alps, as doubtless have you yourself. Ah, *Domina mea*, thou art indeed the snowy Jungfrau and I the tired wanderer. How the Alpine traveler from a great way beholds that white summit in the blue sky ! How his desires go up to it from the dusty pathway of the valley ! Thou art far off like that alluring summit. If I might but rest in thy shadow ! if I might but cool my temples with the touch of thy snows !

The rose, for all the sweetness at her heart,
Droopeth her leaves apart,
That weary wayfarers may breathe her scent
And travel on content.
The thrush, for all the melody he hath,
Singeth above our path ;
And burdened men departing on their way
Still hear him all the day.
The pool that wears the stars upon its breast,
Rears not an angry crest
To mar the mirror ; but all men behold
Its glory, and are told
How in their heart such heavenly lights may
    rest. —

And thou sweet lady-flower,
My bird in leafy bower,
Untroubled well reflecting many a star!
If I but touch thy arm
To still my love's alarm,
Thou wilt not shrink as at a painful jar!
To all the world they lavish
The rapture none could ravish;
And thou, from one who pleadeth in thy touch
Peace to a heart that, loving, suffereth much,
Wilt thou withhold thy charm?

XXVI.

The weather is too hot for long sermons, you
will say, but I feel disposed, nevertheless, to
preach, text and all. About a fortnight ago I
read a sentence in Saint Augustine's "De Civi-
tate Dei" which has been haunting me with the
evil persistence of a ghost that will not be laid.
At the time of perusal the words made very little impression upon me, so little that only their
general purport recurred to me later on, and I am
unable to recall the exact form of their expression.
But now every day when I compose my thoughts
for the night, their profound significance comes
back to me with importunate intensity: "The
gods desire our imitation more than sacrificial
rites." These are not the precise words of the
text, and I have quite forgotten from what old

pagan moralist the Christian father quotes, but their meaning remains.

They have troubled me much: for it is my habit always at the close of the day's labor to con over the thoughts and impressions scattered through the hours, summing up their purport and binding them to the main subject of my meditation; and this pagan sentence, which yet affected me so strongly, persistently remained apart, separate from the general current of my thoughts. You remember how Franklin and other wise men made it a habit every evening to recall in succession the events and talk of the day. They thought thus to strengthen the memory, and retain their past life in the present lest it should quite escape them and time should become no more than a moving point. I have endeavored to imitate them so far, induced, I fear, by the promptings, not so much of orderly wisdom, as of exacting passion; and with this difference, that with me one domineering idea or passion, half suppressed during the day, wakes with the coming of night, and imperiously exacts from each thought and sensation and wandering fancy of the past hours, an answer to the demands, " What service dost thou offer me? what is thy kinship to me? art thou of my imperial army wherewith I march to subdue the barbarous foes of my peace?" — It is with my thoughts as with the antique world: all roads must lead to Rome —

and this Rome is not the capital city of human achievement, nor that ideal Rome of the Christian father which he called the *Civitas Dei*, but a new city, a *Civitas Amoris*, where the great Queen rules. As I began to say, it is my habit always in the quiet of early night to lead back all my reflections of the day to this imperial court, as slaves return from labor at eventide to the home of the mistress whom they serve. Rather is it a collecting and arranging of my thoughts, a putting in order of the chambers of my mind, as a house is swept and garnished when a noble guest is about to enter in — for such a noble guest I call the image which abides with me. At times, however, some single thought or fancy, discovered in a book or born in my own mind, pertinaciously stands aloof, refusing to fall into this well-ordered economy. Such a thought, or cadence of words, merely, it may be, troubles me night after night, provoking reflections which lead far away from the true desire of my heart. But when at last I find some profounder relationship between it and the general drift of my meditations, then the gratification is greater than ever. It is like a discord which heard alone jars on the ear, but being sounded in its proper sequence heightens and fulfils the progress of a complex harmony.

So it has happened with this sentence from Saint Augustine concerning imitation and sacri-

fice. And when, last night, its true connection
with the love that binds together my thoughts
was revealed, immediately I desired to make
some record of my delight, if possible to give to
you some reflex participation, however slight, in
my great pleasure. I could think of no better
method of conveyance than this poem which I
copy within. Be pleased with it for its good
intention.

"IMITATIONE POTIUS QUAM SACRIFICIO."

" By imitation more than sacrifice
   We bind the gods." — Oh, stern idolatry !
And I, who love and worship, in such wise
   Would draw thy favor from thy own sweet sky.

Nay, be assured : beyond each paltry gift
   Wherewith my love would masquerade in
      flowers ;
Beyond each song wherein my brain would lift
   Its weaker flight to serve my heart's high
      powers ;

Beyond it all the larger purpose lurks
   To bend my orbit to thy blissful height ;
By imitation of thy fairer works
   To win thy splendor of serene delight ;

That mortals, looking from their ways of trouble,
May wonder, hearing that our spheres are double,
   How like a single star they cleave the night.

XXVII.

You recollect, *Domina mea*, an exceedingly long time ago, to wit, last Saturday evening, we talked for a while about the immortality of the soul, and you repudiated doubts on that subject as mean and narrow and altogether repugnant to you. I have been thinking about this a good deal since then, endeavoring to find some solace for a necessary evil, recalling to mind the many great men who have labored under the same eclipse — among others Plato himself, whom you mentioned, and who puts a word of doubt into the mouth of his Socrates even as he turns from the judges after his memorable apology. But this is poor consolation, you will say, if the truth remain ; and I am forced to concur. And then the thought comes to one : What if the truth be plain and manifest to all who are not blind within, like the sun visible to all who have eyes ; and this inability to discern the higher things above us arise from some moral turpitude darkening the spiritual vision, some innate affinity to lower and more transitory desires which voluntarily bends the eye downward. Others seem to behold this greater world of eternity, this true macrocosm, as it were a purer and more ethereal sky enveloping our little world. From thence come to them moral light and the vision of other abodes, as the grosser sunlight drops hitherward, so that there is no room in them for questioning. Can a man deliberately blind himself to all this? There are passages in the Bible which seem to say so, and Saint Augustine everywhere declares sin to be the voluntary declension of the free will from a higher good, not to an absolute evil, but to a lesser good, a choosing of the more material light for the true celestial. Or, at least, whether the inability to discern be from choice or from moral impotence, the course of such a one may be like that of a blind man who walks abroad to enjoy the scenery of a fair country. Many individual objects meet him on his way. The grass may be pleasant to his feet; sweet odors attract him here and there; the breeze is as cool to him as to others; the trees rustle overhead and the birds sing from their boughs; he may even feel the flowers with his fingers, and by his touch obtain some notion of the form of various objects on his way, — and yet all the while, the one thing which makes the scene so splendid to others, the light which illuminates the whole and combines all the varied fragments into one harmonious view, giving color and life to the individual objects and transcendent unity of design — this is only a name to him; and the observations and delight of his more fortunate companions must awaken in him something of wonder or even of incredulity. Suppose further that this blind man has spent much of his life studying what others have recorded of

the visual world, their descriptions of sublime
scenery, the mountains and the sea, their sensations and reflections from the view of what to
them must appear as the harmonious work of
some divine artificer, who unfolds in all its wealth
of detail about them one grand purpose of creation — will he not be filled with amazement?
For, as I said, to him if he walks abroad the
world can be no more than a disconnected series
of accidents displaying only occasional beauty
and no design. In darkness like this, you would
claim, the mind may be involved which sees in
the moral world only change and transitory desires, with no light of a future existence to blend
them into one eternal hope. We walk in shadows groping for the way.

Do you remember when Aeneas traverses the
realm of the dead, seeking knowledge of the future
and of the fates of Rome, that he hears voices
telling dimly what shall be, giving admonition and
advice, that he sees the dusky fields before him,
discerns the shadows of men walking about —
Dido among others — as one beholds, or seems to
behold, the new moon through the western clouds?
Do you remember, too, that he meets his father,
who speaks with him as when alive; but that, when
departing he would give the filial embrace, three
times he endeavors to throw his arms about his
father's neck and three times the empty shade
eludes his grasp? The myth is borrowed from

Homer, and may be common to antiquity. I
think it meant to them what it means to me, — a
symbol of that future world of which seers at times
have strange vision, out of which the inspired
seem at times to hear oracular voices, but which
no man can quite grasp with his mind, for it is
after all only the shadow of his own desire : —

> "Heaven but the vision of fulfilled desire,
>   And Hell the shadow of a soul on fire."

Believe me, I have sought laboriously through
the philosophies and religions of many peoples to
find if perchance somewhere or sometime a gifted
race had sure intelligence of this dim realm.
And in the end I must say with the poet, —

> "And all philosophy can teach is *bear*,
>   And all religion can inspire is *hope*."

If I revolt from substituting an intellectual creed
for the beauty of mere hope, you must not cen-
sure me. Of all untruths the worst and most
deadly is, not the falsehood we utter, but the
falseness with which we deceive ourselves, by
which we are fain to rest in easy hopes of
empty persuasion when the truth is hard and
unwelcome. And shall I declare my vision is
clear, when in reality I see only the blackness of
night? Whether I am blind in the day or strain
my open eyes ineffectually in the night, I cannot
know. Let others build their hopes on what
seems to me merely the inner flashing of an

overtaxed eye. And some of us who are called blind have striven very hard for a glimpse of the promised glory, for some understanding of the God whose merciful nature is the pledge of our fulfilled hopes. Jacob wrestled until dawn with the Lord as with a man, crying out, I will not let thee go unless thou bless me! and in the end he received the blessing and was no more called Jacob but Israel, " who had prevailed against God." It was a priceless victory, for which the halting on one thigh was small payment. But how many of us upon whom the ends of the world are come, have wrestled more than one night, crying many times, "Tell me thy name !" and have grasped only shadows, heard echoes alone, and for our vain efforts have gone halting through life, unfamiliar to its pursuits — for the great struggle, though futile indeed, has made the lesser prizes of the world quite despicable to us.

Last night I was walking on the beach, and it was there the notion of writing all this to you came into my mind. The solemnity of the scene, the innumerable waves leaping up into the light of the moon, the stars climbing upward from the water that sparkled as with its own galaxy, the ceaseless motion and the infinite peace, led me to link fancy with fancy. I sat long enough in a secluded spot to weave some of my thoughts into rhyme, giving them the seal of so much labor to prove to you my seriousness. I had intended naturally enough to send you the verses, but find I have already told all that was in them excepting the conclusion. This consisted in a vision of that " Lord of terrible aspect," who appeared to Dante as the Master of the new love that had sprung up in his heart. So this Lord stood before me as if arisen from the depths of the sea, reproaching me for these doubts of mortality, being, as he declared, of too lofty and imperious a character to dwell in a bosom that harbored such vulgar guests. At first, being much abashed and humiliated, I hid my face from his gaze ; but then, plucking up courage at the thought of my true service and of the misericord which this god veiled beneath his terrible aspect, I replied in this wise : All that thou sayest is true, and the loss of faith in the future blessed world does indeed rob this life of its beauty and dignity, leaving it as a corpse from which the divine breath has flown. And yet, my Lord, thou knowest that the doctors of old have defined this word *eternity* to be not unending duration of time, but the complete abolishment of time ; so that our hope of bliss may not depend on a belief in a future that shall succeed the past and present existence, but rather on the attainment of a new state in which all sequence of events shall cease and the soul shall know no shadow of change because absorbed in the contemplation of one unvarying theme. They say that an Angel of the Almighty shall set one foot on land and one foot on the sea and swear that time shall be no more — meaning, no doubt, that the desire and vexation of transitory things shall be swallowed up in communion with the Eternal who shall be *omnia in omnibus.* And so, my Lord, to me, who doubt and may never believe, thou art thyself in this present life, that Angel of the Almighty. Thou hast laid thy commands on my soul, and the fretful desires of time have vanished from my peace. I am rapt up into a vision wherein all the motions and changes of time and space are blended into one supreme purpose, as with the saints the impulses of life are absorbed in the service of God. Great learning I have acquired ; and if the manifold occurrences of the past and varied aspirations of the future are all in thy service wrought into types and impulses of one supreme changeless desire, shall I not say that for me Love has wrought the multiform into the One, has changed time into eternity ; that Love has transcended faith, that Love is very God, and that service to him is now and in this world the immortality we crave ? Therefore, my Lord, be not angry with me ; abide with my soul, that shall serve thee as the Eternal is worshiped in heaven by the ranks of the Cherubim who know, and the Seraphim who love. — At this I raised my eyes, and, behold, a great light round about me !

XXVIII.

I was walking down the Avenue where the Park stretches away to your right, thinking not so much of the objects about me as of a certain other matter, when my attention was caught by a lady just ahead. Whether it was caused by some peculiar effect of the twilight filtering slantwise through the trees, or by the glinting color of her dress, or whether my imagination imagined a vain thing, I shall not presume to decide; but certainly this lady appeared to me to proceed with a distinct glow of light about her. Naturally it struck my fancy and set me to linking odd conceits together; for the soft radiance surrounding her figure brought me to consider what special charm so distinguishes her in my eyes from other women. I thought of a thousand things which you would choose not to hear; and then this fancy came to me, that the love which so many men have lavished upon her, leaving their own lives, I fear, too often dark and meaningless, clings about her as it were a halo of glory, making her path luminous in my sight. It may be this joy, which many have surrendered to her with their love, has bestowed on her life that peculiar fullness of light and beauty which I so often try to describe to you. And then I asked myself, Will this love of mine also render her still more beautiful and desirable to the world, adding

its beam to the lustre that already encompasses
her? The thought pained me at first, as if my
life were to be all in vain. But this trouble scon
passed away and a feeling of great content succeeded. I still wonder how much it is dreaming
on my part, and how much it is true that the love
a man bestows on a woman may add zest and
value to her beauty, waking all manner of fair
and noble thoughts in her mind, flooding her
heart with sentiments of sweet loving-kindness,
and surrounding her body with new effulgence.
Can you tell me how this may be?

Down the wide Avenue my lady went,
  All girdled round with glory for her mark;
  So the gray twilight, drifting o'er the park,
  Flushed in the glow and with her halo blent.
And some one whispering told me what it
      meant: —
  How the dear loves that often bade her hark
  Had left their lords to traverse rayless dark,
  And, hovering o'er her head, this aureole lent.
Then said I, troubled: If she will not hear,
  Shall love forsake me too, and all my light
  Go to adorn her path already clear?
Ah, be it so! yet in my sombre night
  This hope, that I have added to her cheer,
  Shall be the star of morning to my sight.

XXIX.

. . . Last night was the first in my new chamber, and before going to sleep I said to myself, Now let me conjure up the image of my *bien-aimée* so distinct that it will not fade away during my slumber, but bring me pleasant dreams. This will be the christening, the solemn dedication of my new abode, for surely the habitation ought to be made sacred wherein is to dwell the remembrance of so fair a lady. Consequently when the light was out I proceeded to summon up your likeness, beginning with the general form and salient features, one after the other and very distinctly, till the whole person was before me. And then memory called up the little traits which give so much individuality to a picture, — the peculiar bend of the eyebrows like the two wings of a swallow poised in mid air ; the thin nostrils that are wont to palpitate with your breath, when you are excited, as the petals of a white rose tremble in the breeze ; the sea of dimples that flutter all about your mouth and chin when you smile, little roguish white butterflies chasing one another around a red, red rose ; the sharp line your lips make for a little space where they come together at the ends, now bending up and now down according as I please or vex you ; the sharp point dividing the upper lip in the middle ; that ambitious lock of hair which will rise up on

the crown of your head on the right side; the
wretched little curl on your forehead which I tried
to unroll last night, and was slapped for my
pains; the soft *duvet* on the contour of the cheek
like the bloom on a peach or plum — a sign of
beauty, by the way, which I pride myself is unknown to the *profanum vulgus;* the rapid dila-
tation of the pupils of the eyes when — shall I
continue? have I not learned my lesson pretty
well? Try yourself in the mirror to-night and
see if I have perverted or exaggerated a single
point. All these traits and a host of others
which it is prudent not to enumerate here, I pre-
sented to my fancy in minute detail; and then
surrendered myself to sleep, never doubting of
the dreams that should come to me. And what
do you suppose I dreamt? What golden vision
escaping from the shadow world through the epic
gate of horn or ivory visited my spirit? Woe's
me! never a dream did I have all that night.
What we desire most is farthest from us. To be
sure I have some faint recollection of a vision of
white flowers and lucent faces floating above me
in a bright light; but it is all vague, neither do I
remember discerning your form in the throng. It
is not the first time I have failed signally in this
matter, as you know; and I must surrender to a
stronger magician the mercurial wand that has
power to compel the dim shades whither the master will. To revenge myself I passed part of the

day in dreams all of my own concocting, being master of day-dreams at least. Ah, if you could see yourself in the midst of this fairyland that I conjured up! How proud you would become to be queen of so marvelous a domain.

All this was yesterday. Last night again before sleeping I went over the same catalogue of delights, and this time was rewarded with the desired dreams. It seemed to be the smile that most held my fancy. For I thought I was teasing you again, putting my fingers on your eyelids, trying to discover what made your throat smell so sweet, doing a thousand idle things that vexed you almost to despair. And then you looked at me so sadly and pathetically that I felt like a robber or highwayman, and just wanted to be hanged about the neck until dead — your neck, not mine. Some such silly remark made you smile despite yourself, and — why, if one should drop a half-blown jacque rose into the midst of a bowl of sweet milk, the little eddies and ripples in the liquid would be just like the dimples around your mouth when you smiled ; for curiously enough the skin adjoining your lips is the whitest of all your face. After that I suppose I again did something forbidden, for you frowned dreadfully and my dream ended.

That the following whim may not derogate from the supreme dignity of the starlike queen whom I worship, it has pleased me to indite the following lines to an imaginary maiden of more familiar name.

SALLY SMILED.

When Sally smiles, all round her red, red mouth
   A thousand tiny dimples leap and run ;
As when the wind puffs lightly from the south,
   White pools of water twinkle in the sun.

Round the corolla of her lips they dart,
   Or hover where the sweetest honey grows ;
Like milk-white butterflies that meet and part
   In wanton mirth about a red, red rose.

So nimble too, the roguish little elves,
   In vain I 'd merely touch one ere they go ;
Like saucy bunting-birds that flirt themselves
   And revel in a field of virgin snow.

When Sally smiles — but when she pouts for
     anger
Because I 'm bad, they droop in deeper languor
   Than southern lilies if the northwind blow.

XXX.

I went to St. Thomas's yesterday. A voice within me said go, and I went. Dr. —— was in his pulpit, and as you were not in your pew, you shall hear something of his sermon. The text has been ringing in my ears all day: "From henceforth let no man trouble me; for I bear in my body the marks of the Lord Jesus." The word marks is in the Greek *stigmata*, the term used always by the Fathers for the signs of crucifixion in the hands and feet, and the wound in the side. They are thus symbolical of the supreme passion, of the death which He suffered that He might give life. And Saint Paul means to say (I follow Dr. ——) that in his service of the Master he also had suffered, that his body had been buffeted and wounded and his heart lacerated in his witness for the truth; for he had been "crucified unto the world and the world unto him." And then the preacher exhorted his hearers to serve the Lord with this same diligence, sacrificing the pride of the intellect to the simplicity of faith, the lusts of the heart to the hope of heaven, and the strength of the body to the ministry of love. Deprivation and pain would come, the marks of sorrow and isolation would be left upon them, but these would be the stigmata of the Lord Jesus, the blazonment of the hierarchy of heaven. And in the end would be found the peace of God that passeth understanding; and they might say, From henceforth let no man trouble me.

Of course I have not attempted to put down the flights of eloquence that gave life to the sermon, but you can fancy how stirring the dis-

course may have been. Especially it affected
me because it is this very peace that I seek,
wherein no man and no spirit of despondency
may harass me. At one time in my life I was
ready to give up liberty and ambition of thought
in order to become a disciple of the faith that
promised peace in this world and resurrection
in the next; but, thank God, the pride of my
intellect revolted from such a betrayal of its nobler, if yet austerer, aspirations. Let me bear
my bitterest doubts with me to the end rather
than succumb through lassitude to an easy belief
promising repose. It is possible to submit with
the heart when the intellect rebels: it is the abnegation of all that is divine within us, a moral
cowardice not to be countenanced. There are
many who believe without reflection, a few who
are led captive by honest but shallow reasoning ;
there are others who surrender to a creed that
offers hope, because they are not strong enough
to endure the conflict of doubt unto the end.
Ah, if I could bow to this Jesus and serve him,
not with the serenity of the disciple whom he
loved ; but if at least the bitterness and isolation
of my soul could somehow be brought into his
service, transforming the marks of sorrow into
the stigmata of victory! If they could be the
signs of witness-bearing to a great truth instead
of the stigmata of a despair that I am almost
ashamed to uncover before you. But alas! alas!

quid est veritas? we must ask again, and again surrender the Lord to the scoffers of this world.

And then I thought of that other Master unto whom I am willingly bounden; and of the saying, God is love; and of that other saying, Now abideth faith, hope, and love, but the greatest of these is love. It came to me as a new gospel of deliverance. For if I serve faithfully this Lord of love, and to follow after him cast away all sordid impulses and unclean fancies and unworthy desires and mean affections, shall I not have done what that other Lord Jesus commanded? And if amid the temptations which offer fruition in place of devotion, I hold fast to the true love, deeming its bondage better than the liberty of others, shall I not have taken up my cross and left all and followed him? And if in the times of my deepest despondency, when hope and life itself seem a mockery, as they do now and again to many of us, if then I seek consolation and strength in this divinity and he seem to abandon me, promising no fellowship here and no continuance hereafter, shall I not cry out, "My God! my God! why hast thou forsaken me?" Many a man, with no consciousness of divine powers within him to render the desolation less terrible, has uttered these words of the Christ. And if he still keep faith in his Master and blaspheme not, shall not the marks of his passion be the stigmata in which Saint Paul

gloried ? And with these stigmata on his hands
and in his side he may say in truth, From henceforth let no man trouble me. For what to him
are the cares and temptations and fretful hin-
drances of this world, who bears within himself
the victory of an undying passion and the devotion which in austere service finds eternal rest ?
He likewise has discovered that peace of God
which passeth understanding.

XXXI.

Let me add a postscriptum to the note I sent
yesterday. After writing as I did, I went out
for a short time to court the night breezes before
retiring. The day had been wet and disagreeable, but now a fresh wind had blown up and
cleared off the air. The sky was covered with
shoals of white clouds drifting across it from
west to east. Above them the full moon, very
white and without any halo, hung like a lamp
in the vault of heaven. And as my eyes fell
from the sky above to the outstretched sea mur-
muring at my feet, with its innumerable white-
caps seeming but a reflection of the clouds overhead, my mind instinctively wandered back to
Homer and the myths of the Greeks, to the picture
of Achilles wandering forlorn by the many-sound-
ing sea, and of his mother, Thetis, the silver-
footed daughter of Nereus. It seemed to me I

could see the fair nymph racing naked on the
shore of one of her Ionian isles, where the long
rolling waves of her father's realm broke on the
sand at her feet, and scattered the white spray in
a mist about her whiter shoulders. How like she
must have been to the argent moon scudding
through the breakers of heaven. I could see her
hair streaming out on the night air, and hear her
voice challenging her sisters to follow in the race.

Then it all changed, and the image of the moon
was a fair new Phœnician vessel, decked with the
silver image of Astarte at her prow, and dashing
through the stormy channels of the Cyclades.
The long tiers of oars, bending under the efforts
of the slaves to stem the current, made the water
about her flanks foam up whiter even than the
breakers tossing on the rocks. I could hear the
song of the sailors chanting to the goddess under
whom they sailed.

But too soon, alas! my thoughts wandered
from the happy scenes of old to the sterner reality of my own present. My heart was too full
of what I had been writing and meditating;
and this pageant above me became the very
symbol of what I sought, a pretty answer to
my query decked out in the metaphors of celestial poetry. The clouds drifting in confused
masses, putting on and off innumerable fantastic
shapes, were emblematic of this world of phenomena that perplex our vision with ever recurring

and disappearing forms, without intelligible design or order save that they all rise out of darkness, are beheld for a moment, and sink back into
the same oblivion. And the radiant orb above
them with her serene countenance was the sign
of that idea of beauty which I seek everywhere
in the world, that principle of harmony which
Plato dreamed of, and which would make the fair
objects about us not mere toys of pleasure jumbled
together by chance as in a kaleidoscope, but
bearers of some celestial purpose, perishable
vapors themselves perhaps, but glorified in vision
as they pass beneath that splendid orb of truth
which they veil indeed, but whose light they reflect far into the darkness. — If it were only so!

And shall I tell you what came next into my
mind? Have I not told you before? It is what
Dante would say, — only in his way, in his way.
The doubts returned. It was as if in that cam-
era of my brain where the sky was pictured, an
east wind with fog and mist-rack had blurred
the images and veiled them over. And then I
thought of you, and again my heart sang within
me for gladness. For I said, let doubt under-
mine the very pillars of the world, let there be
no God, no eternal life, no moral purpose; let
the realities about me become the merest phantas-
magoria of my own imagination, the thin shadows
cast by the light of my own burning heart, fair or
hideous as my moods shape them — doubt can go

no farther than that, no man's doubt has ever brought him lower than that : yet will I bear within me the likeness of one fair woman, whose beauty and loving-kindness shall rest upon these fleeting images and whiten them to the whiteness of snow. Around this one radiant thought of her, all thoughts and imaginations, and joys and sorrows, shall circle in order. Then shall virtue become, as Augustine calls it, *vera ordo in amore.* I will not look where the horizon gathers the darkness, but only above whence her glory drops upon me. This was the happiest fancy the moon suggested, and immediately I turned homeward lest some duller imagination should supplant it.

And now does it seem to you strange to be so spoken of ? or has the homage of many men made it sound familiar in your ears ? You will say that I have idealized you, that the light I discern is the work of my own love. Be it so. The image in my heart remains unaltered, and I have gained what many might covet. Yet I deem this is not all. There is no such faculty within me, no such light, only gloom : the glory must be all your own, Esther. My love is vision, that is all; and it is my chiefest pride that this inner eye of the soul is pure enough and strong enough to descry clearly what would only dazzle the multitude. Often I tremble lest somehow you should deprive me of this vision by withdrawing the light; as if my love did itself in some way spring from you and depend on your pleasure, and that troubling your peace it might be withheld. My love is only vision, and if the light be withdrawn, I know not what salvation shall come to me in that utter darkness which is death. — I have finished my postscriptum.

XXXII.

Very carelessly I neglected to put the violets in my last letter, so you will have to find time to open two envelopes instead of one. This gives me a chance, however, to send you the enclosed sonnet. Pardon the boldness of a mad poet.

A summer noon we loitered by a brook;
   And I, to win her shy lips oftener,
   Whispered, " Oh, but she knew how fair she
      were
   When kissing — kiss me, dearest, whilst you
      look ! "
She smiled, and, leaning o'er a waveless nook,
   Half turned her mouth. — Ah me, the mirrored
      stir
   Of lilies round her flower-face lovelier
   Bewildered so, that kiss I never took.
Even then, how frail, I thought, the shadows rest
   On troubled streams that wander to the sea,
   How fair and still on so untamed a power!
In such a wise her beauty in my breast,
   Above the tide of passions as they flee,
   Shall brood serenely like a mirrored flower.

XXXIII.

. . . What touched me most, however, was the attitude of a young Jewess sitting desolate on one of the miserable stoops of Mott Street. She sat quite still, with one arm supporting her chin and the other hanging listlessly over a basket at her side. Her face was inexpressibly beautiful, perfectly pure, with just the faintest shadow of suffering on it to foretell the ruin that must fall. She remained motionless as a picture, utterly regardless of the noisy altercation of two men, apparently Irish, who stood on the steps above her. Her mouth was delicate as a queen's, and the lips, slightly puckered from the pressure of the hand on which she leaned, seemed to me to express both weariness and disdain. Her eyes were cast down, and she did not raise them in the slightest although I involuntarily stopped before her. She appeared oblivious of everything about her, as if brooding on the great mystery of her life. My first thought was of the Madonnas I have seen portrayed in the galleries of Italy; and this unknown Jewess stood before me as the embodiment of all the dreams of the centuries, the living image of the inspiration which those artists wrought upon their canvas. And then I wondered what she was brooding upon, and whether her beauty was to her also a delight, or rather troubled her consciousness with its

weight of mysterious responsibility. Did she
realize the value of this possession which, handed
down in the world from one woman to another,
has always been to mankind the enduring sign of
the incarnation of his God, — this moulding of
inert matter into the spiritual forms of loveliness, which must appeal to men as the indwelling
of the divine puissance, and as the emblem of the
eternal love that pervades the world and that
has been fashioned by religious instinct into the
legend of an incarnate virgin-born God ? Did
the vague shadow of such a thought trouble her,
making this beauty of hers a sacred and awful
thing to be borne through the shocks of her rude
life ? I suppose not. Some nearer grief weighed
upon her, or some more definite foreboding. And
yet, feeling as I do the higher significance of
beauty, I often wonder what burden of possession
it brings the owner. You could answer me this
if only you would. Is this superlative grace also
but a shadow, the work of chance, a mere pheno-
menon of the surface ? or does it arise from some
interior necessity, and is it the expression of a
spiritual indwelling power ? And certainly if it
be the emblem of such a controlling force, some
intimation thereof must abide with the owner,
some intuition, vague perhaps, of the god within
him who so clothes himself in corporeal grace. —
But you are silent; I walk in a world of silence;
and fear seizes me lest it be the silence not of
choice but of necessity.

A FAIR JEWESS.

In Mott Street, crouching on the ruined stoop,
  She sits and broods her womanhood complete,
With brow leaned forward and tired lids that
      droop,
  Unmindful of the rabble of the street.

Some new-born wonder makes her more than fair;
  As if reflecting in her virgin bloom
How one, for comeliness, was said to bear
  The Lord of human triumph in her womb.

Ah, might she dream that beauty such as hers
  Bears still the incarnate Christ whom we im-
      plore!
Or is it fear, the shadow of a curse,
  To trail this fragile flower from door to door?

Of all the glory of our Empire City,
This image follows yet with tears and pity
  For something lost that will return no more.

XXXIV.

I send you the Indian epigrams of which I
spoke. Strange, is it not, that these Hindus, of
all peoples in the world, should display the greatest shrewdness in their epigrammatic verses.
From the windows of their silent abstraction they

were yet able to cast piercing glances into the
world of action about them.   The verses that follow, however, do not, so much as others I might
have selected, exhibit this phase of their understanding, but hint rather at the deeper spiritual
insight which forms the true wisdom of the east.
In this, I begin to suspect, must lie the consolation
of those who find our western religions superficial
and our philosophies mechanical; for here is
taught in its purest form the method by which
the individual soul, shaking off the trammels that
bind it, may mount upwards unto true communion
with its infinite source.

I.

Unworthy be the toil-polluted world of sense,
Ay, hateful as the camping ground of all offense;
   Yet even in the truth-devoted heart, anon
Bursts forth its   vast unnamed impetuous ve-
     hemence.

II.

Life like the billow rolls, and youthful bloom
   Finds in a day its doom;
Wealth fleeter is than fancy, pleasure's lash
   Is but the lightning flash;
And those dear arms that hold our neck, beguile,
   Ah, but a little while; —
Rest then the heart in Brahma till we cross
This sea of being where all perils toss.

III.

These dear Companionships are not forever :
The wheel of being without end
Still whirls. If on the way some meet ánd
    sever, —
'T is brother, mother, father, friend.

The words of this last stanza do not begin to
convey the force of the original. In it is concen-
trated the very essence of Indian pessimism,
a pessimism, however, whose shadow is quickly
dispelled by spiritual illumination. The soul
whirls ever onward through its wearisome round
of existences, passing through innumerable
forms of life. If here and there we cross the
path of some other soul in our breathless flight,
it is for a moment father, lover, friend to
us. Not in such transitory connections is our
hope to be found, but only in the rest and
oblivion which some day may cause the spinning wheel to pause in its course, to be forever
still.

IV.

The following stanza will show that delicacy of
feeling is not excluded by this pessimism. Often,
indeed, the tenderness of Hindu poetry brings it
much closer to us than the sterner sentiment of
the classics. Here we have a romance all in a
few lines : —

" Why, pretty fool, art thou so slender grown ?
Thou tremblest ? and the prize
Of all thy roses, wherefore is it flown ? "

" My Lord, it meaneth nothing," she replies,
And smiles, — but when alone,
Loosing the tears up-gathered in her eyes,
Poor fool, she sighs and sighs.

v.

Fire is the Brahmin's god ; the seer
Knows in his heart the godhead near ;
Fools have their idol ; but the clear
Untroubled vision sees him there and here.

vi.

Alone each mortal first draws breath ;
Alone goes down the way of death ;
Alone he tastes the bitter food
Of evil deeds, alone the fruit of good.

vii.

Out of the substance of our thought
All that we are is shaped and wrought.

viii.

You have read in the Buddhist scriptures of
the temptation and victory of the Exalted One.
For seven weeks he sat beneath the Bo-tree
wrapt in meditation. Mara, the tempter, with

his army that stretched twelve leagues before him and twelve leagues to the right and left, and behind him reached to the rocky limits of the world, — Mara with all his host assailed the Exalted One, hurling against him storms of stones, and ashes, and burning coals, and all manner of deadly weapons. Yet the meditations of the Exalted One were not disturbed nor his body injured. And when at last a great light shone upon him and he beheld the four excellent truths that were to save the world : The truth of sorrow, and the cause of sorrow, the release from sorrow, and the way of release ; — then flags and streamers were seen suddenly to wave from horizon to horizon across the sky, blossoms burst forth on every tree, the ten thousand world-systems revolved like whirling wreaths of flowers, light shone in the void places of the universe and in the depths of hell, the water of the seas was sweetened, and among men the lame and deaf and blind were made whole. Then the Exalted One became omniscient, the enlightened Buddha ; he knew that the end was near, his course was run, and the spirit, freed from the evils of repeated birth, had attained to the blessedness of Nirvana. Then it was the Exalted One uttered this song of triumph, which in the countless cycles before him each preceding Buddha had pronounced in like manner at the moment of his enlightenment : —

Through many births, a ceaseless round,
I ran in vain, nor ever found
The Builder, though the house I saw, —
For death is born again, and hard the law.

O Builder, thou art seen! not so
Again thy building shall arise;
Broken are all thy rafters, low
The turret of the mansion lies:
The mind in all-dissolving peace
Hath sunk, and out of craving found release.

XXXV.

. . . As for my work, I am doing none — in
the way of composition, at least. The very
word is a mockery to me. I have nothing to say
that were not better unheard. Do you remember
those lines : —

" Yet why evoke the spectres of black night
    To blot the sunshine of exultant years ?
Why disinter dead faith from mouldering hid-
        den ?
Why break the seals of mute despair unbidden,
    And wail life's discord into careless ears ? "

I am satisfied if I am able to wring out, here
and there, some pleasing simile, or find some bond
of union between my love and the appearances
about me, which I may sing, as best I can, to

ears that are not quite "careless," thank God.
That high ambition which I builded so fair — of
what use is it to me, since the proud guest for
whom it was erected disdains to abide therein?
It is but a crumbled palace, a broken arch, ruined
before ever the key-stone was set in place. Ask
me not, dear Esther, for work that Love will not
suffer me to perform. If you read Greek, you
would remember the famous words in the Epistle
of Saint Ignatius: "Living I write to you, but
desiring to die. My love is crucified, and there
is within me no more fuel for its fire, but the living water speaking in me and within me saying,
'Come!'" Is this what you would have me say?
There is no strength in me both for love and the
inspiration that saith, "Come!" If love must be
crucified within me before I can obey the high
summons — why, then, let the work wait for another.

But I am looking on the gloomier side: the
bitterness of regret for all that love might have
ennobled and made radiant causes me to see
only the darkness of its failure. Give me yet
more time to become master of myself, and it
may inspire instead of crush.

You ask me if there is nothing better in the
world to love and worship than a woman. There
is not. I am not a follower of Jesus. I do not
know his God, cannot find him, do not hear his
voice. The great self-abnegation and passion of

Jesus seem to me often a greater mistake; for what blessing has he brought to the world? To miseries which he cannot alleviate he has added only the further miseries of sympathy. I am not a disciple of Dante. His vision of heaven and hell has passed away forever. His faith is a thing outworn. The new vision must somehow be a justification and glorification of the life that is bounded by the narrow walls of time. My eyes are too dim to discern this glory; there is too much of darkness within me. And yet, at times when the thought of you is most vivid, when love comes to me as something from without and above, I do catch glimpses of this vision which make the heart within me leap up for delight. It is the transfiguration of love. It is the image of a beautiful body so strongly imprinted on the eye that all objects are tinged and made radiant by it, and come in some way to strange relationship and similarity thereto, acquiring transcendent loveliness. It is the belief in a moral beauty so firmly implanted in our mind that all the relations of life are colored by it, and the motions of the spiritual world fall into harmony as if circling about this mighty central idea. Such a love may in these days be the revelation we have so long sought in vain. There may be a "refined sort of selfishness in it." It may absorb the world in the individual rather than dissolve the individual in the world. Yet the consummation is much the same, and this is the selfishness which in the end must save the world, if there be any salvation. And at the last, it may be found in some unforeseen way to include the higher abnegation.

XXXVI.

Dear girl, when in thy evening orison
  My name is murmured and my peace implored,
I know the prayer; for, with its triumph won,
  Going the long, long way to seek the Lord,

It weareth yet thy form, all white-attired,
  As spurning other semblance than thy own:
And the proud Seraphim and ranks inspired
  Will listen, while it pleads before the throne.

I know the prayer! Here in the darkness now
  It leans above me, pausing on the way;
So near, I feel its breath fall on my brow,
  And see the dear lips moving as to say: —

"Behold, the fears that made thy worship falter,
I bear them with me to God's holy altar,
  A sacrifice; love only while I pray."

And while I was turning these verses over in my mind, the story of one of the old Fathers recurred to me, who needed not to pray in as much as his whole life was absorbed in unceasing communion with God. It is the most beautiful encomium ever pronounced on a Christian; and the desire awoke in my heart so to bear my Master ever in my thoughts that my life may become in like manner a continual communion with this Lord of Love. Surely into that fellowship "the cares that infest the soul" will not dare to intrude; and the intermittent exaltation and depression of life, the prayer and the silence, will be wrought into the serenity of unbroken worship.

XXXVII.

Disagreeable duties took me into the heart of Gotham to-day. The turmoil of the place had stunned my ears and bewildered my brain, and finding myself near the enclosure of Old Trinity, I turned in thither for relief. The coolness, the quiet, and the gray shadows of the church were only the more impressive from the indistinct murmur of the streets that now and then penetrated the closed doors. After resting there for a time I went into the old God's-acre, always to me the most solemn spot in the world, here in the midst of our noisy Gotham. It is a place sacred to Death, set apart at the confluence of two mighty streams of life, where Wall Street empties, as it were, its human current into the greater flood. I looked out through the tall fence upon the surging multitude as one might look upon the eddies of a

river from which he had been rescued, and the
words of the poet came to my mind : —

"Suave mari magno turbantibus aequora ventis,
  E terra magnum alterius spectare laborem."

Touched by the quiet around me I wondered at
the unrest and the eagerness stamped on the faces
that jostled by.   What a little thing it was which
stung each of them and urged him on ! no better
than the gadfly which drove Io pitilessly over the
world ; what a paltry thing which, if obtained,
must be so soon released.   My brain dizzied at
the thought of these countless beings ever pouring
past in their vain pursuit ; nay, of the infinite hosts
that stream through the ways of the universe
ages without end.   Is there anywhere respite
for the soul ?   I wondered whether the Hindus
were right after all, and from birth to birth we
are hurried through an innumerable series of
existences, never at rest, seeking some ultimate
goal, we know not what.   And these forms that
rolled past the bars of my enclosure, what were
they ?   The visible world and the invisible became confused, intermingled, in my mind.   I
thought of the strange fable of the Buddhists concerning the Pretas, the restless dead who wander
in the outcast purlieus of the world-systems, or
haunt the scenes of their former life, never pausing in their headlong career for a space .longer
than the snapping of the finger.   They are thin

and withered like dried leaves; they are aflame
with the fires of inextinguishable fever; they are
consumed with unappeasable hunger and thirst.
Somewhere I have read in the Buddhist books
the legend of a priest who entered a great city
to search for a certain Preta, having obtained by
virtue of a medicinal herb the ability to discern
these wandering ghosts. And so numerous were
they, thronging the thoroughfares of the city, that
his progress was blocked and impeded by them.
It seemed to me now that by some perversity of
fate this vision was given to me, and the hurrying
eager multitude of the street were but shadows
of humanity, unreal things seeking an unreal good.
Who shall say that the unseen dead do not flock
through our cities, leading over again in shadow-
wise their former lives ?   Who shall say that to
some they are not visible, jostling against the
living amid the crowded streets in the very light
of day?

And then I turned to the crumbling monuments
about me that seemed to mock my fantastic musings.   How sombre is this place in the shadow of
the lofty walls, how still ; and I think that those
who rest here have found for themselves the
shadow of a great rock in a weary land.   Truly
some shall find rest.   The ancient tombstones
peer out on the heedless crowd rushing by and
silently protest against the bustle and change and
importance of mortal affairs.   At the noontide

and evening, when the street is in a turmoil, the unearthly repose of the spot strikes one with something of mockery. How idle appear the petty ambitions lashing themselves about this place of eternal sleep. And in the night hours just before dawn, when the noise of the city has died away and belated men look questioningly at each other as they meet, then the solemn hush within this enclosure fills one with unspeakable awe. The shadows of night drift past us on the silent pavement, and we say they are the souls of the generations before us who trod this same way in their life, whose desires and ambitions, suffering them no respite, bind them still to walk with us this fatal valley. But some of them are gathered by day, I think, into this old God's-acre with their brothers who wander not.

The dust settles unmolested in this home of dust, the rain falls more softly here, and the snow rests for a season pure and white as if to cover the dead with its spotless sheet. However urgent my business may be, I always pause here an instant, touched by the pathos of the scene; and a wonder comes over me at the thought of those slumbering so silently beneath the clamor of this busiest thoroughfare of the world. And as I pursue my way, something of its solemnity abides with me and tells me my place is there with the dead, for the living have other cares than mine. My heart also is a burial place swept by a ceaseless tide of human thoughts. Here lie buried hopes dearer than life, wrapt in the long slumber; love has quenched his torch in this dust; and the fires of passion have shrunk into these ashes; sorrow even and remorse have mingled with the general oblivion; and here the brawling voice of ambition is muffled by the earth. *Resurgam in pace* is graven on the marbles over those who rest in the cemetery, but for the dead in my heart there shall be no resurrection. No earth-born son of the Almighty shall descend into this silent abode, waking them into new life. Their epitaph shall be *requiem aeternam.*

It is fitting, too, that this spot should have special significance for me. Here strangely enough the light first came, which led me into this new life of peace. For must I attempt to conceal it from you any longer? Already you have divined the change that has come upon me. The consummation of my hope is near; my heart has found the mystic haven of rest. Some prophetic import lay in the finding of love here where all the passions of men are quieted, a premonition that love should lead me, not into the fullness of joyful possession, but into the more abiding fullness of renunciation. For love is crucified within me, and henceforth I listen only to the divine voice speaking from the infinite calm of the heart.

How well I remember : it was two years ago,
just about this season of the spring, that I stood
by this same monument looking out on just such
a scene as this. There was bitterness in my
meditations. To satisfy my parents I had been
working that winter, teaching Latin to boys; and
day by day the conviction had been forced upon
me that such a life was worse than death, was
beyond my powers of endurance. I began to
learn that any active life among men was for me
impossible. I knew not what it meant, I knew
not where to turn. Mere idleness would seem to
my people a disgrace. The enigma of existence,
of my existence, pressed upon me ; it seemed to
me I must there and then solve the fatal problem
or lose my heritage of being. The men of the
street upon whom I looked out seemed in some
way the cause of my mental torment. It was to
satisfy their ideals that the dream-life of my soul
must be roused into painful activity. Their facti-
tious world of daily routine and sordid cares bound
my spirit as in an iron chain. I began to hate
them. As always happens with me, my vision
was affected by my emotions, and the stream of
faces that flowed past became like so many dia-
bolical apparitions, distorted, grimacing, threaten-
ing. The rumor of their voices and footsteps
became like the noise of a tumultuous victorious
army charging over me. I waited in suspense ;
something was to happen. And then, suddenly,

as I thought, a great hush succeeded; their voices ceased, their footsteps were muffled. They parted to the right and the left, and between them, as down an avenue, moved a Lady, silent, looking ever before her, majestic, radiant beyond telling. Ah, I might relate marvelous things that flashed through my mind at that apparition, legends of fair women of old, who by reason of surpassing beauty trod unharmed amid the uproar of the elements, or walked amidst evil men and ravenous beasts free and untouched. It was only a minute, and then I hurried through the church and out on Broadway, determined at all hazards not to lose this glimpse of joy from my life. But already she had passed on her way; the sordid throng pressed about me. I sought her along the street, but in vain. I even questioned one or two loiterers, but they were amazed at me; they had seen no such vision. At last I went home, dejected, doubting not that this also was a picture of my imagination. The actual world became accordingly still more hateful to me. My despair grew intolerable. And then, just when I thought all was over, I met my Lady Esther, and she was the Lady of my vision. That was two years ago. Since then life may have been dark at times; yet always a star shone in my night: until now, guided by the sweet influence of that celestial sign, I have found the night more grateful than the day. Sleep cometh with

the night. And while others toil in the heat, I
shall have found slumber and peace.

XXXVIII.

The philosophy of India, the wisdom of the
east, may be summed up in three mystical words.
He who knows them, knows all; he has attained
to the end of learning. These three are Brahma,
Atman, Om. Bear with me a little, Lady Esther,
while I unfold to you something of their meaning. It will be to tell you all that remains of my
life.

Brahma signified originally the swelling of the
heart in the fervor of prayer, the feeling of exaltation which ever comes to a man in seasons of
earnest worship, when the walls of his personality are broken down and the infinite powers of
the universe sweep over him. At such times
the soul knew of the God that encompasses the
barriers of the senses, and the word describing
the condition of the worshiper was naturally ex-
tended to this nameless power with which he
communed. So this God was called Brahma,
the infinite, eternal, unchangeable, all-embracing, all-pervading. And he who in times of
ecstasy felt his spirit rapt into communion with
this God was said to know Brahma. And as
knowledge with the Hindus, and forsooth with
all men of insight, is a manner of identification,

and what we know, with that we are made one;
so he who knew Brahma was said to be united
with Brahma, to be Brahma.   Our Jesus meant
no more than this when he said, *The kingdom
of heaven is within you;* and when he avowed
that *I and my father are one.*

The Atman is much the same thing, and generally in the books the two words are inter-
changeable.   Yet in their beginnings they were
distinct.   Brahma is the divine power grasped
from without; Atman, the same power grasped
from within.   Atman is the breath, the breath
of life, and thence easily enough life itself.   It
is the anima, the soul, the spirit.   It is what remains when everything else is stripped away; it
is the inmost being, the *Self.*   It was the aim of
those forest-dwelling philosophers who gave up
the world that they might surrender themselves
to uninterrupted meditation, it was their aim to
penetrate through the outer trappings of man's
nature into the secret places of the heart.   And
there they found this Atman, sitting in solitary
state, a king hidden from the gaze of the idle,
passionless, unmoved, while the faculties of the
mind and the organs of the body, like ministers
of state, served his bidding.   And then looking
out upon the world they perceived a similar
power dwelling in the innermost shrine of nature, a higher Self to whom this natural world
was what their bodies were to them.   And while

the ignorant were busy trafficking with the phenomena that were the mere underlings of his
court, they put aside these things that their Self
might hold converse with him, the greater Self,
Paramatman or simply Atman, as they called
him.   And again, as he who knew Brahma
became Brahma, so he who knew the Paramatman was raised into union with it; and Brahma
and Atman were but different names of the one
Spirit.   This conception of the inner and the
outer Self, and their essential unity, is undoubt-
edly the ultimate achievement of thought.   And
this is clearly to be distinguished from a philosophy that would exalt the individual *Ego* of a man.
For the *Ego* says within us, *this is I! this is
mine!* and is but a fiction of the brain, rising
and perishing with the body : but the Self is pre-
cisely that within us which is least individual,
which suffers not nor enjoys, which knows neither
birth nor death, which is not a portion or emanation of the Eternal, but is that eternal Self.

It is related in one of the older Brahmanical
books that a certain king of Benares disputed
with a Brahmin, or priest, concerning this
Brahma from which the priest held his title.
The priest offered many illustrations to set forth
its mystic meaning, but always the king replied
that this he knew and still more.   At last the
priest had to confess his ignorance; and then
the king mocking him, took his hand and led

him apart to where a man lay in deep sleep. And with this example before them he taught the priest the true nature of Brahma: how the soul, when the man wakes, is distracted by the jarring of material and intellectual existences, so that, forgetting its home in the Great Spirit, it surrenders itself to a thousand transient cares: how then when the man slumbers, the soul escapes from this concourse of gross phenomena, and builds for itself a new shadow - world of dreams, and there it magnifies the joys of its former state a hundredfold; yet still is not contented, being as it were a mature man playing with a child's toys: and how then leaving this realm of dreams it passes into deep sleep and is there at rest, being united with Brahma, its original source and home.

Thus the divine life of man may be compared with the temple of a god. In the outer courts is the bustle of commerce, the changing of money, the driving of herds to the sacrifice: but within are the worshipers kneeling before the altar; while above them and around them rise the fantastic images of the gods; and over all floats the fragrant cloud of incense, so that he who enters seems to move in a dream: yet all this is for the vulgar; still beyond lies the holy of holies where only the anointed priests may tread; they draw aside the curtain and enter in, and falling on their faces wait for the coming of the god : here is no idol; here is nothing to meet the eye; the chamber is empty save for the awful presence that abides therein.

To signify this spiritual experience the Hindus had a single word, OM. Perhaps the term originally expressed only a strong affirmation, like the Hebrew *Amen.* But from its liturgical use it grew to include for the devout the fullness of his faith and worship. Yea, it said to him, yea, it is all true. I too am one with the Atman, my spirit has gone out into fellowship with Brahma. What mortal care shall trouble me henceforth? *Om! Om!* The very sound of the syllable carried blessings with it, a sound to exorcise the doubts of the heart, having efficacy to lead it upward through the three stages of spiritual progress into the desired haven : for so is the progress of the soul divided, as was explained ; and so is the syllable *Om* made up of three corresponding elements, O being a diphthong composed of the vowels A and U.

Now they say the first letter, A, because of its Attachment to all other letters and because it is the first among them, is no other than Vaiçvanara, the god who rules over all this visible world and over the waking souls that are bound therein. He that knows this shall have the might of Vaiçvanara; he shall attach to himself all desires, and be first among men.

And the second letter, U, because of its Uplifting or because it comes between the other two, is Taijasa, Lord of the dream-world and of them that sleep yet dream. He that knows this uplifts the train of his ideas and becomes passionless.

And the third letter, M, because it is the Measure of the others or because they enter into it, is Prajna, Lord of the domain of deep sleep. He that knows this is himself the measure of this universe; he enters into all things and becomes all things — he that knows this, that knows this.

But the fourth, they say, is not a letter at all, but the whole syllable *Om*, the incommunicable, absorbing into itself this visible expansion, benign, above duality. He himself by himself enters into the Self — he that knows this, that knows this. —

And I think now, Lady Esther, you know what I wish to say, and the harshness of my message is softened. You know better than any other what the struggle of my life has been. Perhaps mine has been the most unfortunate of human temperaments. A mind that always doubts, united with an imagination that continually reaches after the infinite and finds no abiding place among transient things, — such a union must form a most unhappy disposition. What my searching has been, how I have striven to find peace in the common faith of men, you know only too well. I have boasted that through the intensity and breadth of my love for you I would build up a faith in beauty able to bind the physical with the moral world, and to content my heart. But you have understood my words expressed more an ideal than a reality, and have wisely held my love as a thing fair but insubstantial. The completeness of your life will not be endangered if this is withdrawn from it. The beauty of your life will suffer no real detriment if you do not see me again.

However sudden this decision may seem to you, yet it is inevitable and has been well premeditated. Of late I have pondered much, walking by night among the crowded streets of the city, if perchance inspiration might come to me from the atmosphere of humanity; and again walking in solitude here by the sea, " that wilderness where sing the servants of God." And ever one word sounded through all my thoughts — one word which is the key-note of one of the great Indian philosophies, *Kaivalyartham, for the sake of abstraction, isolation,* sounded in my ears above all the uproar of the city; and again *Kaivalyartham* was the admonition borne to me from the turbulence of the sea. That philosophy teaches us of the duality running through all, and of the soul that abides in the body as a prisoner in his cell. By ignorance of this duality we are held in the bonds of flesh. But the wise man, having knowledge of himself, strives after abstraction from the things of the earth ; and in the end Nature, like a dancing-girl who has once been seen, withdraws herself from his vision. The play is played out ; the illusion is dispelled ; and he that has been spectator of it all silently departs to his home. This is the final message for which all my life has been a preparation. Henceforth my way must lead through the solitudes of abstraction and meditation ; no human care shall touch me more. What neither Christianity nor philosophy, neither art nor science, neither love nor friendship, has been able to afford, that I have found in the mystic *Brahma,* in the *Paramatman.* Some unusual fate has brooded over me from my birth. I have gone through the waking world of men as one walks in his sleep. I have not understood their words, nor the springs of their actions, nor their joys and sorrows. I have not bowed the knee to their god Vaiçvanara, who drives our souls hither and thither in his blind service. Hitherto my life has been a dream. In the temple of Taijasa I have reveled in fantasies, insubstantial as clouds, gloomy at times, and again radiant with the splendor of the sun of love. Yet I have not found rest. It was but the pageantry of evening that precedes the night. Now I would enter into the silence of communion that is likened most unto deep sleep. I am warned that the period of life remaining to me is very precarious. Death will be a change only in name. — And so good-by, dear Lady; you have indeed been the evening star to usher in the peace of night. May greater love than mine surround your path with still purer light.

XXXIX.

I took down my copy of Leopardi this evening to recover in memory that apostrophe which tells, you know, how sweet is.

"Il rimembrar delle passate cose!"

I had not read in the volume for many months, yet as I opened it now the leaves of themselves parted at the splendid ode to *Il pensiero domi-nante;* and reading that, I forgot what I came to seek. Long use had accustomed the book to open there; and besides, a bunch of withered vio-lets had been pent up all those months with the transcendental verses, and were pining to escape. Poor things, they were simple children of mother earth, and bore about them once all the sweetness of the woods. They had little sympathy with the poet's lofty disparagement of earthly beauty and his contemplation of the *angelica beltade.* And yet in the mind of another, — not a poet indeed, for no joy came to him with his visions, — these same meadow-flowers were intimately bound up with his almost equal devotion to that *angelica beltade.* He was not a poet, I repeat,

but one so seduced by the witchery of meditation that often he could not discriminate between
his aspirations toward the celestial beauty where-
of he too went conversing with his thoughts, and
that other *finta imago* which a mortal woman
bore upon her countenance. Do you recollect
that one springtime you sent me in a letter from
Washington a cluster of purple violets? That
was the first time you ever wrote to me, and you
said — but you must remember the words. That
epistle was my magna charta, my title of nobility.
The season was late with us in the north. Only
the little spring-beauties were dancing in the
woodlawns; and after reading your letter I went
out and gathered a few of these to send in reply.
But at night when I had written my answer, the
little beggars had all gone to sleep with their
heads tucked away as tight as you please. I sent
them as they were, however, with some silly
verses apropos, which you perhaps never read.
You have forgotten the verses, and the little
spring-beauties went the way of other flowers : —

> "Où va la feuille de rose
> Et la feuille de laurier ! "

But your violets suffered a better fate at my
hands. And to-night the finding of them has
brought me back for a time into the world I have
left, and set me to linking together memories
delle passate cose.

How many other flowers are scattered here and there in my library, flowers you gave me on parting, or which it may be I nefariously purloined. They are with me yet, pressed in whatever book I chanced to be reading at the time. Therefore am I pleased to call these dusty bookshelves — for, alas, they are dusty — my garden, and would not exchange it for all the greenhouses of Long Island. And from this garden to-night I will gather every blossom that grows, and send them to my Lady. Let her prize them; I shall never again send her flowers.

Yonder stands my yellow-backed Montaigne, and turning the pages I find a dry stalk of narcissus — strange lodging-place for the daintiest of flowers. They were favorites of yours always; and that evening while you read aloud to me, I plaited a golden circlet of them, twisting together their long stems; and then, setting it on your head and kneeling at your feet, proclaimed you queen of my days. You were pleased with my folly, and untwining one of the stalks pinned it on my coat. Now it rests here among the mocking essays of Montaigne. Almost I can smile as I think of the strange incongruity of it. And yet, *que sais-je?* what questioning of love's celestial hopes even then sent me for sympathy to this subtle skeptic? Narcissus, we are told, pined away from too much gazing on his own loveliness: love also may fade from too fond consideration of its sweetness. He may yet prove wisest whose philosophy teaches merely to laugh with the present.

It seems as if some angel of perversity had arranged the setting of my garden. Here in the first chapter of Daudet's "Sapho" lies a sprig of heliotrope, sweetest of plants. I cannot recall when or how you gave me this, yet here it is ; and I read once more the page telling of the young *provincial* and the strange burden he carried up the long flight of stairs. What melancholy event could have brought me then to this book that I had read so many times ? I take out the heliotrope with a feeling almost of shame. No, my burden was not like this.

I am astonished to discover how many of these volumes are freighted with dear memorials ; the record of all my evenings in your presence is written in these perishable hieroglyphics. In my Virgil is a single purple aster. One afternoon in the still autumn weather we walked together over the Jersey hills. And while we were resting beneath the shade of a pine-tree, I read to you the wonderful sixth book of the Aeneid. Do you remember that in our enthusiasm we said this poet must endure long-lasting as the world, for he more than any other wrapt about his song the mysterious atmosphere of Fate, of the great world overshadowing our little life. As we parted that evening you gave me this one purple

aster from your girdle. And now always, whenever I wander with the Roman exile in the regions of fate, this flower awakens recollections
of a hope that like a star made the shadow of
Virgil's spirit-world less awful and less intense.

Merciful heavens forfend! Out of this tremendous folio of the *Acta Sanctorum* falls a tiny
spray of lilies of the valley. Ah me, once before
they fell to the ground, torn from their resting
place near your heart, when in my impetuous
folly I had caught you in my arms. And you,
to hide your embarrassment perhaps, slipped out
of the bonds and stooped to gather up the fallen
flower. The expression of my eyes must then
have warned you that I was about to claim it as
my own by conquest of arms, for you tossed it to
me and ran. I saw you no more that evening.
The lilies have lain since then in this ponderous
work of the Bollandist Brothers. I look now at
the open page and a marked passage catches my
eye. It is the account of that terrible angel who
visited Saint Theresa, and the learned Brother
interprets her words : *Videbam illum longum
quoddam jaculum aureum, sed ad ferri cuspi-
dem pauxillo igne inflammatum, in manu ha-
bere : hoc ipso ille cor meum subinde ad intimas
usque fibras transverberare, et, dum illud rur-
sus educeret, quaedam earum frusta simul edu-
cere videbatur : quo facto, ingenti Dei amore
me totam aestuantem et inflammatam reliquit.*

Tam vehemens porro haec poena erat, ut in hos me gemitus et expostulationes faceret prorumpere ; sed suavitas quam summus hic dolor mihi adfert, tam excessiva es ut eum mihi auferri prorsus nolim, nec anima minorem voluptatem ac delectationem quaerat quam ipsummet Deum. Further on it is related of her that by the vehemence of this *amor Dei* her soul was withdrawn not only from the senses of the body but even from the body itself. And the chroniclers add in justification of this that many pious men have died from the same cause. I remember on the day I was reading this narration that I vowed my earthly love should resemble this celestial passion. It seemed to me a magnanimous life to surrender all the faculties of mind and body to one such master desire, to fling one's self into the current of events and wrest from them wealth or renown as the fit adornment of beauty. At times I may even yet regret the contest in such an arena for such a prize. But my strength has been exhausted in a struggle with other foes than men, and my passion has evaporated into the clouds of mysticism. It is too late for repentance.

Here are other flowers a-plenty, roses and carnations and lilacs. Last of all I take up my Hebrew Bible. I pause for a moment guessing what memento may be within. I open the volume and turn the pages anxiously, as the mussulman consults his Koran for an oracle. In the

very heart of the prophets I find a rose, once
scarlet, now fast turning a dusty gray. That
day, quite contrary to your habit, you wore on
your breast one of the roses I had sent; and from
that sweet garden it came to wither between the
pages of this crabbed Hebrew — a sad change.
Yet glorious are the words of the prophet, the
most sublime in the world. I have learnt them
by heart in many languages: the vision of Isaiah who "saw also the Lord sitting upon a throne,
high and lifted up." This is my oracle, and I
reflect with melancholy interest how once it was
indeed to me the voice of God. For it happened
that same evening that we stood, as I was about
to leave you, talking of the vision I had seen in
my boyhood: — how one summer afternoon as I
sat by my window overlooking the treetops, suddenly the design of a great work had flashed on
my mind, a poem which should portray the long
conflict of humanity, the war between the personal will and impersonal law, the contest of
doubt with faith, the opposition of centrifugal
inert matter and central force. As champion of
this struggle was Cain, the seed of the serpent,
who should pass reincarnated through generation
after generation to appear finally as the Wandering Jew; while arrayed ever against him was
Jesus of Nazareth and the long line of prede-
cessors; until at last reconciliation came in sub-
mission to all-controlling, all-embracing Fate. —

Thenceforth my life appeared sacred; I bore within me a new oracle to men. I told you how I had held to this vision through all the circuitous imaginings of later years; and of the burden that weighed on me to proclaim my message unto the world in fitting words, if possibly some who heard might be led to take up arms in the spiritual warfare. I told you of my burning ambition to sing as never man had sung yet, of the longing that left me not while the body slept, that fatigued the spirit and isolated me among my fellows. And then I told you of my doubts, of the radiance of celestial things that blinded my eyes, of my weakness, my ignorance, and unworthiness: and "Woe is me!" I cried out, "for I am undone; because I am a man of unclean lips, and I dwell in the midst of a people of unclean lips: for mine eyes have seen the king, the Lord of hosts." You were as if caught up in my own enthusiasm; and, leaning forward quickly, you kissed me on the mouth, and said, "Love hath touched thy lips and they are made pure." After that I took the rose from your breast, that it might be, I said, a remembrance to me of what had happened, inasmuch as the live coal from the altar had touched my lips. Naturally that night in my chamber I opened to the familiar chapter, and read again the vision of Isaiah, and closed the book, presuming to say also: "Here am I, send me."

Years have passed since that night, and the message that pressed upon me so is still unspoken — nay, shall never be spoken. Wisdom has trod upon the heels of knowledge, and what seemed to me the divine voice sounds now poor and human. Possibly another service has banished the earlier one, and the worship of the new God demands silence. Or it may be, some feeling that the song I should sing must be a mystic utterance, a speech *amanti verbum non mundum*, mingled with fear of the world's scorn, has kept me dumb. Certain it is that the season and the power of utterance have passed away; and if any regret comes to trouble the repose of my new life, at least it is not the regret of ambition : —

> "Inveni portum : spes et fortuna valete ;
> Nil mihi vobiscum : ludite nunc alios."

Duty itself has no more claim upon me. There is no duty in peace. And it is ever for those who have not found Peace to publish her to the world. —

Here are all the flowers of my garden, Lady Esther. You will prize them, will you not, for the plants may not blossom again.

XL.

The mighty Brahmin Vajraçravasa, to win peace for his soul, would offer up all that he had. So the sacrifice is made. But while the cattle

are distributed among the priests, faith enters
into his son Naciketas, though a mere boy, and .
he thinks :

" Barren and worthless are the cows my father
bestows ; never more will they drink water, nor
eat grass, nor give milk, nor bear calves. They
are called joyless spheres to which the giver of
such attains."

Therefore he spoke to his father : "Father,
here am I ; to whom wilt thou give me ? "

And, because his father gave no answer, a
second and a third time he said : " Father, to
whom wilt thou give me ? "

Then Vajraçravasa was vexed and replied :
" I give thee to Yama, the Death-god ! Go,
dwell in his house for three nights ! "

And because the vow of a Brahmin bears its
own fulfillment, therefore the boy Naciketas,
with the life of this world still upon him, departs
to the realm of death, to the gloomy mansion of
Yama. And while he sits in the great hall by
the portal, waiting, for the master is away, he
questions the Doorkeeper who also sits waiting :

" Sir, I come the first among many ; I come in
the midst of many. Tell me, what is the master's pleasure that he will do with me to-day ? "

But the Doorkeeper only replies : " Look
backward into the past, look forward into the
future : as it fared with them that went before,
so shall it fare with them that come after. Mor-

tality ripens and falls like the corn of the field, and like the corn of the field springs up again."

So for three days the boy sat in silence, waiting the appearance of the god, meditating these dark words.

And when at last Yama returns, his Doorkeeper chides him, saying : "Like the presence of sacred fire is the advent of a Brahmin guest to a man's house. Therefore men ' salute him and order water for his feet. Surely from the host who offers not meat and drink to such a guest, from him shall be taken hope and expectation and friendship, truth and sacrifice and pious works, children and herds."

Then Yama was troubled and saluted the boy Naciketas, and said : "O worshipful Brahmin, three nights thou hast been a guest in my house, neither has meat nor drink been offered thee. Hail to thee, and may it be well with me! Choose now three boons, one for each night."

And the boy said : "O God of death, let my father be appeased; and let him know me and receive me graciously when thou sendest me back to him. This is my first wish."

And Yama replied : "As of old shall thy father have pleasure in thee when I dismiss thee hence out of the jaws of death. Peaceful shall be his sleep, and his trouble shall be assuaged."

Again the boy said : "In the realm of heaven there is no fear. Thou art not there; neither does old age nor hunger nor thirst nor pallid care bring dismay to the dwellers in that celestial sphere. By good works, it is said, we may attain that joyous life; and thou, O Death-god, knowest what sacred fire leads upward to this heaven. Teach me that fire, for I have faith. — This is my second wish."

And Yama replied: "I know what fire, O Naciketas, leads up to heaven, and I will tell it thee. Behold, it burns in the secret place of thy heart; behold, also, it glows in yonder eye of the world. It is Agni, who before the beginning of the spheres flamed forth out of the depth; Agni, whose passing smoke is the body of these realms of migration. As are the stones of the altar of Agni in number, so are the days and the nights of thy year. As the flames of the sacrifice mount upward into the empyrean, so the fire of thy devotion in good works bears thee aloft to the gods."

"And because thou art faithful and quick to learn, therefore shall this fire henceforth be called by thy name, Naciketas, *that is beyond thought.* — Ask now thy third boon."

Then the boy said: " When a man dies there is doubt amongst us whether he continue or whether it be all over with him. For it is said the god Dûr may carry his speech across into fire, and it again becomes fire; may carry his breath across into the air, and it is air: that even so his eye returns to the sun, and his hearing to the four quarters of space, and his mind to the moon.

"Of his good and evil deeds new actions arise. They take unto themselves name and form, they clothe themselves in a subtile and a grosser body, and a new creature is born.

"Yet we know not if the very Self of the man endures, passing onward from birth to birth, unchanged, invisible, unknown, unto the great consummation. Tell me, does the man altogether perish with death?"

And Yama replied: "Even to the gods this was long ago a matter of doubt. It is not easy to discover; it is a subtile nature. Choose another wish, O Naciketas; urge me not, but release me from this boon!"

And the boy said: "Because, as thou sayest, O Death-god, this matter was a doubt even to the gods, being hard to discover, and because there is no teacher to be found like unto thee, therefore is no other boon equal to this boon."

And again Yama replied: "Rather ask for thyself sons and grandsons who shall live a hundred years; choose cattle and elephants, horses and much gold; demand for thyself great estates and long life. Ask whatsoever thou wilt; choose riches and length of days, and wax mighty upon the earth! I will make thee to know the pleasure of thy desires. Call upon me for the delights of this world that are hard to get, chariots, all instruments of music, and women divinely fair. Only ask not concerning death."

But the boy said: "These, O Death-god, are the cares of mortal man, that endure till the morrow, that dull the edge of the senses. Yet our whole life is but a little time. The world itself and all the spheres of the gods do wax and wane away. Keep thy chariots, the singing and the dancing. Riches may not satisfy a man. Shall we hold fast to our riches when we descry thee? Shall we indeed live while thou reignest? I abide by my wish. I have no other desire than that which searches into the dark secret."

Then at length Yama made answer and said: "There are two things that engage men, though their ends are diverse. One thing in this world is the good, and another thing is the pleasant.

"Both the good and the pleasant draw near to men; but the wise man proves them and makes decision. He chooses the good among these, and it is well with him.

"But fools for their welfare's sake choose what is pleasant; yet they fail of the end. They are wise in their own conceit, puffed up with vain learning; they run about in the paths of illusion, being blind men led by the blind.

"Thou, O Naciketas, hast pondered these pleasant-seeming desires and made renunciation. Thou hast not turned into the road of wealth where many go astray.

" Far apart are the paths of knowledge and illusion. Thou hast chosen knowledge for thy portion, O Naciketas: the pleasant things of the world have allured thee not.

" Thou wast come upon the attainment of human desire; all the joys of this life were thine; moreover thou sawest before thee Agni upon whom the worlds rest, the sacred fire whereby the celestial spheres are won : yet all this thou hast renounced ! "

And the boy said: " Yea, I renounce! But that which is above the good and the evil, which is beyond the create and the increate, which is more than what has been and more than what shall be, — thou seest that, and that thou wilt proclaim to me."

And Yama continued: " My child, we call it Brahma, the Great God; we call it Atman, the Spirit that is within thee and about thee, the Self that is within thee and above thee.

" It is hard to discern, unfathomable, hidden away from vision, concealed in the depths, in the secret place of the heart.

" It is neither begotten nor does it die. It proceeds from none, and none proceeds from it. It is unborn, eternal, omniscient, the Ancient of Days, perishing not with the body.

" If the slayer think he slays, or the slain think he is slain, they know not.

" Sitting still it yet wanders afar ; lying at rest

it yet runs hither and thither. It is joyful and without joy, bodiless in all bodies, changeless in all change.

"The spirit that wakes in those that slumber, fashioning unto itself joy upon joy, this is that pure Brahma, and is called immortality. Upon it repose all the spheres, and no man may go beyond. This is that.

"There is a deathless holy tree, whose roots strike upward and whose boughs descend; this is that pure Brahma, and is called immortality. Upon it repose all the spheres, and no man may go beyond. This is that.

"All this world, whatever is, trembles in that living breath; it has come forth and stirs with life. It is the great awe, the uplifted thunderbolt. In awe thereof the fire burns; in awe thereof the sun burns; in fear thereof the Great Gods speed, and I, the Death-god, with them speed.

"As the one fire pervading the world takes innumerable forms, so this Atman, abiding in all things, takes innumerable forms — and is yet without them.

"As the one breath of heaven pervading the world takes innumerable forms, so this Atman, abiding in all things, takes innumerable forms— and is yet without them.

"As the rain that falls on a mountain-top is scattered and poured down in many rivulets, so is scattered the soul of him who discerns not amid

the shifting changes of form the one Atman.   He
runs hither and thither ; he is born in the flesh,
and dies, and is born again.   He finds no respite.

"Like pure water poured into pure water, so is
the soul of him who sees and knows.   His spirit
is poured into the Great Spirit wherewith it is one.

"Who knows the Great Spirit, the Atman?
who has seen it?

"It is not to be found out by study, nor by
the understanding, nor by much learning.   It
descends freely upon whomsoever it lists.

"It comes to him whose conduct is pure, who
has found peace, whose heart is set upon it.

"And he, the seer, when he discerns that ancient secret Self and has parted therefrom all the
semblances of the world, lo, he is now become
a god suffering neither pleasure nor pain.

"He is rapt into a new joy, and a new peace
that is above joy.

"For shall he know sorrow who as in a mirror
has seen in himself the Great Self, who knows
that the senses, rising and setting again, have no
portion in his Self?

"Who shall tell his peace?

"He is as one liberated in a land of slaves.

"He seeks not to defend himself from any evil
thing, for the Lord of all the worlds inhabits
within him.

"He has trodden beneath his feet both good
and evil.

" He is made one with that which is without beginning and without end.

" There is henceforth to him neither past nor future. He is loosed out of the jaws of death.

" Yea, when all the heart's ties are severed, then already the mortal has put on immortality.

" When all the desires of the heart cease, then already the mortal has put on immortality ; he is come unto Brahma. This is the sum of wisdom." —

" May He preserve us twain, may He profit us ; may we work a good work, may our knowledge prevail; may no enmity come betwixt us twain ! Om ! peace ! peace ! peace ! "

. . . .

I have been tempted to send you this paraphrase of the book which more than all others speaks the true spirit of the Orient, and which in these latter days has come to be the guide of my meditations, my psychopompos. I say " tempted " because, after the separation of these three months, any message from me may seem almost an impertinence. Receive it as a confession, if you will, the utterance of which gives final release to my soul. The rest is silence.

FINIS.

www.ingramcontent.com/pod-product-compliance
Lightning Source LLC
Chambersburg PA
CBHW021118020726
47500CB00003B/818